how2become

Achieve 100% Series How To Study: Ace Your Grades

www.How2Become.com

As part of this product you have also received FREE access to online tests that will help you to pass your exams.

To gain access, simply go to:

www.MyEducationalTests.co.uk

Get more products for passing any test at:

www.How2Become.com

Orders: Please contact How2Become Ltd, Suite 14, 50 Churchill Square Business Centre, Kings Hill, Kent ME19 4YU.

You can order through Amazon.co.uk under ISBN: 9781911259312, via the website www.How2Become.com or through Gardners.com.

ISBN: 9781911259312

First published in 2017 by How2Become Ltd.

Copyright © 2017 How2Become.

All rights reserved. Apart from any permitted use under UK copyright law, no part of this publication may be reproduced or transmitted in any form or by any means, electronic or mechanical, including photocopying, recording, or any information, storage or retrieval system, without permission in writing from the publisher or under licence from the Copyright Licensing Agency Limited. Further details of such licenses (for reprographic reproduction) may be obtained from the Copyright Licensing Agency Ltd, Saffron House, 6-10 Kirby Street, London EC1N 8TS.

Typeset by How2Become Ltd.

Disclaimer

Every effort has been made to ensure that the information contained within this guide is accurate at the time of publication. How2Become Ltd is not responsible for anyone failing any part of any selection process as a result of the information contained within this guide. How2Become Ltd and their authors cannot accept any responsibility for any errors or omissions within this guide, however caused. No responsibility for loss or damage occasioned by any person acting, or refraining from action, as a result of the material in this publication can be accepted by How2Become Ltd.

The information within this guide does not represent the views of any third party service or organisation.

Contents

Introduction 9
General Study Techniques 15
Additional Learning Styles 51
Getting Started with Your Revision 57
Exam Techniques and Preparation 87
Improving Your Memory 117
Memory Games 129
Conclusion 171
Useful Resources 175

Introduction

Welcome to *How to Study: Ace Your Grades*. As the name suggests, this guide will serve as a comprehensive tool for learning how to study effectively. In this book, you'll receive essential tips on the following:

- How to find your learning style;
- Which revision methods suit your learning style;
- How to create a revision timetable;
- How to keep yourself focused and motivated;
- How to make best use of mock exams and mark schemes;
- How to perform well in the exam room;
- How to avoid and reduce stress;
- How to improve your memory.

When preparing for exams, all of the above are important things to consider, and how well you tick all of these boxes will dramatically affect your results. It's important to take them into account before starting your revision.

This book will take you through the entire revision process, from finding out your learning style to sitting the exam itself. Following each step carefully will improve your chances of scoring a high grade and allow you to reap the benefits of it.

Why Should I Revise?

You might have heard the phrase 'failing to prepare is preparing to fail', basically stating that people who do

Introduction

not revise should expect to perform poorly. While this isn't universally the case – some people 'wing it' and manage to do brilliantly in exams – it holds true in most circumstances. Preparation is possibly the most influential factor in your exam performance. No matter how smart you are, preparation will unlock your true potential and allow you to get the best marks possible.

In the past, you might've got away with coasting through exams. While this is certainly more relaxing, it incurs a lot of risk. If you're serious about the opportunities that passing your exams will bring, you'll take the time to prepare. For example, if you're planning on becoming a train driver, there are numerous tests you'll have to sit. If you're passionate about your goals and want to achieve them, you'll take the preparation and revision processes very seriously indeed.

As we'll see in this book, preparation takes several forms outside of revision. It also involves maintaining a healthy diet and a good sleep regime. In addition, any respectable preparation will also involve writing and sticking to a revision timetable. All of these – and more – will need to be taken into account. This can seem like a lot at first, but that's exactly what this guide is for.

Who is this Book For?

Previous books in this series have focused on specific levels of study. In particular, we've focused on GCSE and A-Level preparation and revision, with specific advice on how to approach both.

In this book, the approach is a bit different. Instead of

focusing on a single level of study, we'll be taking a look at tips and techniques which can apply to any exam. This means that, if you're taking exams in the near future, the contents of this book will apply to you. Whether you're taking your GCSEs or university entrance exams, A-Levels, the National Police Assessment Centre, or any other kind of knowledge-based exam, this book has you covered.

How do I Use this Book?

This book will act as a guide to every step of the exam preparation process. Each chapter covers a different part of the road to achieving exam success, and should be read in chronological order.

Here's a brief summary of each chapter:

General Study Techniques

In this chapter, you'll learn about the three main kinds of learning: visual, aural, and kinaesthetic. You'll have the opportunity to find out what kind of learning style suits you best with our learning style quiz. After that, we'll be taking an in-depth look at revision methods for each learning style, so you can get some ideas on how to conduct your own revision.

Additional Learning Styles

This chapter will look at even more learning styles, so you can better identify what kind of learner you are. This chapter will focus on physical, logical, social, and solitary learning.

Starting Your Revision

Once you know what kind of learner you are, you can go about preparing your revision. This is the part of the process where you gather any resources you need for studying, including flashcards, dictation machines, revision podcasts, and more. In this chapter, we'll be tackling the early stages of revision – such as how to create a revision timetable and how to get yourself motivated. From there, you'll learn how to stay focused while revising, so you can work for longer.

You'll also learn how to make best use of mock exams and mark schemes. We'll be telling you where to find them and how you can incorporate them into your own revision scheme.

Exam Techniques and Preparation

In this chapter, we'll be taking a look at tips to help you in the days prior to your exam, as well as what to do while you're in the exam room. This covers what to do on the day, how to plan, and how to get your timing perfect in the exam. This chapter also discusses stress – what it is, how to identify it, and how to deal with it.

Improving Your Memory

This chapter focuses on how to train your memory to be as good as it can be. This is important because having a strong memory allows you to store more information in your head for when it comes to the exam. In this chapter, we'll take a brief look at how memory works, followed by tips for improving it.

Memory Games

After learning how to improve your memory, you'll be given the opportunity to play some memory games to see how good your short-term and long-term memory are. This chapter will also include solutions and answers, so you can see for yourself how you've done.

General Study Techniques

Before getting into your revision, making a timetable, or doing practice questions, it's important to figure out a few things first. In particular, you want to know what revision methods work for you. This is important because finding the most effective revision strategies that suit you, will make studying much easier and much more efficient. Working hard is very important, but it's also important to work smart. By this, we mean that you should focus your efforts on revision techniques that make the best use of your time.

In this chapter, we'll be focusing on the following:

- The 3 different kinds of learner: visual, aural, and kinaesthetic;
- Revision strategies for each learning style.

The Three Types of Learner

There are three major ways that people revise and absorb information. These are:

- **Visual Learning** – This involves using visual aids such as note-taking and creative mapping of information, to commit things to memory.
- **Aural Learning** – The use of videos, music or other recordings to allow information to sink in.
- **Kinaesthetic Learning** – Using activities involving interaction to remember key details (such as flashcards and revision games).

Different paths will work better for different people, but

also bear in mind that certain subjects will also suit these methods differently. For example, Maths may be better suited to visual learning than aural learning, because mathematics (sums and equations) is more visually-oriented than other subjects. However, certain rules or formulae could be learned by placing notes around your study space, if you're a kinaesthetic learner.

Essentially, you will need to experiment with different styles in order to find which ones best suit you, but you will also need to discover which works best for what you're studying for. In the next three sections, we will examine the different methods of learning in more detail. Additionally, each method will be paired with the subjects and exams which best suit it, as well as how to identify which style matches your own.

The quickest way to figure out what kind of learner you are, is to think of what works best for you when trying to remember something. When someone needs to explain to you how to do something, what sinks in the best? Do you learn by watching others doing it first, or by listening to their explanation? Alternatively, you might learn best by giving it a try yourself. Use the following quick guide to figure out what kind of learner you might be:

- **Visual** – You learn best by watching others or reading information. If you're learning a technique in a game, sport, or other activity, you would prefer to watch videos of others doing it, watching people do it in real-life, or by reading explanations. You might also learn from looking at images or diagrams.

- **Aural** – Listening is your preferred style of learning.

You would rather ask for and listen to directions rather than look at a map. If you were learning something new, you'd rather listen to an explanation and follow the instructions.

- **Kinaesthetic** – You learn by doing things rather than just listening or reading. Rather than being told how to do something, you try to do it yourself. You prefer practical, energetic ways of learning as opposed to the traditional methods of reading, listening and note-taking.

General Study Techniques 19

Learning Style Quiz

The following learning style quiz can be used to figure out which of the above learning styles suits you best. Once you're done, head to the answers section, where all will be revealed!

---
1. If you were watching an advertisement for a product on TV, how would you most likely react?

A) You'd notice the imagery, colours and other things happening on screen. ✓

B) You'd recognise and listen to the music, and maybe even hum along if you knew it well enough.

C) You'd remember a time when you saw or interacted with the product in real life.

---
2. You're using a programme on your computer and can't figure out how to perform a specific task. How would you learn how to do it?

A) Watch an online video tutorial of someone doing it.

B) Ask someone to tell you how to do it.

C) Attempt it yourself until you figure out how it's done. ✓

20 How To Study: Ace Your Grades

> 3. If you had to learn lines for a theatre production, how would you do it?

A) Sit down with the script and read your lines in your head. ✓

B) Read the lines out loud to yourself.

C) Get together with a few other people and act out your scene(s).

> 4. You need to remember someone's postcode, so that you can find their house. How do you best remember it?

A) Visualise the letters and numbers.

B) Repeat the postcode out loud to yourself. ✓

C) Write it down.

> 5. You're doing some fairly simple mental arithmetic. How would you solve the sum?

A) By visualising it in your head.

B) By saying the numbers and the operation out loud, step by step.

C) By counting or subtracting on your fingers, or by using objects nearby (such as counting pens and pencils). ✓

General Study Techniques 21

> 6. Which of the following would you most likely do for fun?

A) Watch TV.

B) Listen to a radio show or podcast.

C) Play a video game. ✓

> 7. You're queueing for a theme park ride and the wait time is quite long. Which of the following would you most notice whilst in the queue?

A) The decorations in the queueing areas. ✓

B) The music or sound effects playing in the background.

C) How long it's been since you last moved in the queue.

> 8. If you saw the word "apple" written down, how would you react?

A) By visualising the word "apple" in your head. ✓

B) By saying the word out loud to yourself.

C) By imagining things related to apples (cores, pips, trees, etc).

22 How To Study: Ace Your Grades

> 9. You're in a new place for the first time and need directions. What would you do?

A) Find a map and follow it.

B) Ask someone for directions. ✓

C) Keep walking around until you find the location for yourself.

> 10. When you meet a new person, what do you remember the most?

A) Their face. ✓

B) Their name.

C) What you did with them, or what you talked about.

Now that you've finished, you can find out what kind of learner you are:

- **If most of your answers were A**, then you are a visual learner. You learn by using your eyes to analyse diagrams and notes.

- **If most of your answers were B**, then you are an aural learner. Spoken words sink in best, so you do well when listening to yourself or others.

- **If most of your answers were C**, then you are a kinaesthetic learner. You study best when getting involved and doing things for yourself, rather than watching or listening.

Remember that you don't necessarily have to fall into just one of these three categories. A wide range of learning methods might work for you, so it's good to keep experimenting to find out which techniques suit you best.

In the next few sections, we will cover the three main styles of learning, so you can get some top tips on how to study efficiently!

Visual Learning

Visual learning is exactly as it sounds – you learn by visually representing information, or by having information visually represented for you. This can involve pages of notes, mind maps, tables, animations, slideshows and more. All of these can be used to make information easy to digest visually.

While modern computers are adept at note-taking and mind map making, you might find it more helpful to ditch the laptop for a while and use a pen and paper. This way, you can improve your handwriting skills, make notes which are available at any time, as well as avoid distractions which come too easily whilst on a computer connected to the internet!

Visual learning is excellent for any subject that has a lot of written text to digest, where a passage of information needs to be dissected to find the most important parts. Note-taking can condense a whole chapter of dates, facts and figures into a page or two. Mind maps are a great way of connecting loads of key facts to a single core concept, such as an event or an important person.

Additionally, videos and slideshows are excellent for representing data in a clear manner.

Visual learners tend to be good at remembering images and charts. They'll likely find it easier to remember details of pictures and photographs, and might perform well in memory games where they have to spot which object has been removed from a collection. For this reason, visual learners are suited to organising their revision materials into diagrams, which they will likely find easy to remember.

Depending on what you're studying for, you'll have a huge amount of information that you need to retain for the exams, regardless of what subject you're revising. Some of the following visual learning techniques, such as note-taking and mind maps, are excellent for storing large amounts of information.

Note-taking and Summarisation

This method is exactly as it sounds: you write down notes based on the information in your textbooks or lesson materials. The goal is to collect all of the vital information from your resources.

Use the following steps to take notes effectively:

1. Read through your textbook and other learning materials once, without making notes. Do this so that you get an overall understanding of the material.

2. Go back to the start of the material and begin to re-write the key details in your own words. Alternatively, if the

General Study Techniques 25

book belongs to you, you can underline key points.

3. Continue re-writing important details until you've finished a whole chapter. Make sure to organise the bullet points into sections.

4. Once finished, read over your notes.

5. Then, turn your pages of notes over so you can't see them, then try to remember as much as possible.

6. Repeat this until you're able to remember all of your notes without reading them.

How you go about writing these notes will depend on what you're studying and which techniques best suit you. One way to help notes stick in your head is to underline the key words from sentences in your text books or other materials. Once you've done that, you can lay them out in your notes. This is beneficial because it separates the important details from the less important ones. For example:

> "One of the <u>key themes</u> of William Shakespeare's 'Othello' is <u>jealousy</u>. <u>Iago warns Othello</u> of jealousy being a <u>"green-eyed monster,"</u> and ultimately <u>it's Iago's exploitation of Othello's jealousy</u> that leads to <u>Othello's downfall.</u>"

By underlining all of the key information, we can now organise the facts from the above paragraph into something easier to remember:

- *Key theme = jealousy*

- *Iago warns Othello of "green-eyed monster"*
- *Iago exploits Othello's jealousy*
- *This results in Othello's downfall*

This method allows you to organise information succinctly, so when you return to read it later, you can absorb the vital facts and leave everything else out. By limiting yourself to these facts, you can focus on the details which are necessary. This is useful because you don't want to overload your brain with long, clunky sentences when all you need is the important stuff. What's important is that you transfer the notes into an easily digestible format.

For longer pieces of text with more vital information, you may need to write notes in full sentences. This can be a great way to improve your handwriting and writing skills. The other beneficial part of this method comes in the form of re-writing the information in your own words. It may be tempting to fall into the habit of copying information word-for-word; you might even find yourself doing this without thinking about it. If you're doing this, you're probably not internalising the information, and you might not even understand it properly. There are plenty of machines capable of copying things exactly, but that doesn't mean that they understand the information that they're making copies of! So, you should prove that you understand what you're reading by turning it into your own words. For example:

General Study Techniques

> *"One of the key themes of William Shakespeare's 'Othello' is <u>jealousy</u>. <u>Iago warns Othello</u> of jealousy being a <u>"green-eyed monster,"</u> and ultimately <u>it's Iago's exploitation of Othello's jealousy</u> that leads to <u>Othello's downfall</u>."*

This could become:

> *"<u>Jealousy is the main theme</u> of 'Othello'. In the play, <u>Iago warns Othello that jealousy is a "green-eyed monster"</u>. In the end, <u>Iago takes advantage of Othello's jealous nature</u> and this results in <u>Othello's downfall</u>."*

Here, the meaning of both texts remains largely the same. However, by writing the work in your own words, you are demonstrating to yourself that you have identified the key parts of the text and understood them. Writing information in your own words is a great way to test your comprehension of the text; if you're able to sum up the message of the paragraph in your own words, then you probably understand its content quite well.

Although writing notes allows you to read over them later, the key part of this process is writing them in the first place. When you turn notes from a text into your own writing, you're committing it to memory. Reading it afterwards may be helpful in the short-term, but actually writing it sinks into your head more easily, and it's more likely to become part of your long-term memory.

Visual learners also benefit from making their work more vibrant and striking. This can be done by using different text sizes or colours. For instance, you could write more important words in larger text so that they stand out more. So, when you return to read your notes, you'll see the vital details immediately.

> *"Jealousy is the **main theme** of 'Othello'. In the play, Iago warns Othello that jealousy is a "**green-eyed monster**". In the end, Iago takes **advantage** of Othello's **jealous nature** and this results in **Othello's downfall**."*

Different colours could represent different things in your work. For example, if you were given a text including the pros and cons of nuclear energy, you could highlight the positive parts in green and the negative parts in red. Then, you could use a colour such as amber (or orange) to show important details which aren't necessarily positive or negative.

This traffic light system can be used in all sorts of ways. If you were reading a poem for English Literature, you might notice different themes. The main (most important) themes could be highlighted in green, less important themes can be highlighted in amber and then the least important themes could be highlighted in red.

Finally, you can write your notes as tables if it suits the topic. This is particularly useful for making note of 'for and against' parts of your course. For example, a student revising for Religious Studies might make use of the following:

Euthanasia: For or Against?

For	Against
It gives individuals the chance to die with dignity and relatively little suffering	The right to die might turn into the "duty" to die at a certain age to prevent strain on health services
Legal euthanasia treats individuals as sensible people with personal liberty	In some cases, the individual might not be in control of their mental faculties and might not understand the situation properly
Less terminally-ill people in hospitals will free-up resources for people who can be treated and/or cured	Potentially de-values human beings just because they are ill, might make society less willing to help the elderly and terminally-ill
Prevents a terminally-ill person from becoming an emotional strain on the entire family	One could argue that it's against God's will to end someone's life

Note-taking is a great technique for any kind of learner to make use of, but it's certainly most beneficial for visual learners. For some people, note-taking is the foundation for all of their revision, and they use other activities to simply break up huge chunks of writing notes over and over. It can certainly be monotonous, but it's a tried-and-tested method that lots of students have made use of.

Note-taking: Pros and Cons

Pros	Cons
Simple and often effective	Can be a strain on the hands after long periods of writing
Doesn't require anything other than a pen, paper, and textbooks	Can be incredibly monotonous
Can be used to practise handwriting as well	
Leaves you with pages of notes that you can read more casually	
Re-writing information shows you understand it better	

Mind Maps

Another great way of visually representing your notes, is by creating mind maps. These are webs of ideas and information connected to each other, to show how they are related. Generally, a central concept appears in the centre of a page, and then other details spread away from it. This is excellent for quickly jotting down all of the information you can remember, and then organising it into sections. Take a look at the following example:

Mind Map - *Othello*

- The foundation of Othello and Desdemona's relationship is passion, not love
- Othello believes that love in marriage takes time to develop
- Desdemona's platonic love to Cassio is misinterpreted by Othello as sexual love

- Desdemona's father sees Othello marrying Desdemona as theft of some kind of property
- The mixed-race marriage between Othello and Desdemona would've been unusual and likely the target of prejudice and scrutiny
- The two married women in the play (Desdemona and Emilia) are wrongfully accused of adultery

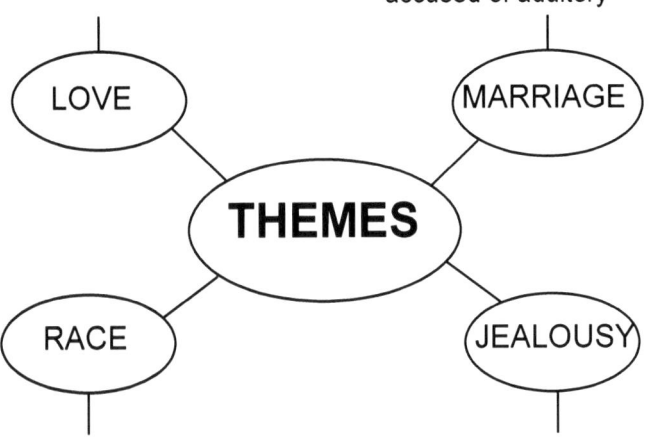

- Othello is a black man in a high position in the Venetian military, which would have been unusual for the time
- Iago uses suspicions about Othello and Desdemona's mixed-race marriage to his advantage
- Othello has internalised some of this racial prejudice, believing himself to be unworthy of Desdemona's love

- Iago warns Othello of jealousy being a "green-eyed monster"
- Iago himself has experienced jealousy via his relationship with Emilia
- Othello's jealousy clouds his judgement, despite him once being a calm and collected individual

Mind Maps: Pros and Cons

Pros	Cons
Can be made by hand or on a computer	Not effective for some subjects, such as Maths
If done by hand, can be a great way of improving handwriting	Has the potential to be less efficient and more time-consuming than other methods such as note-taking
Forces you to write incredibly concise notes, which is great for remembering	Not necessarily an excellent method if you aren't particularly creative
Excellent for subjects with lots of connected events or concepts	
Allows you to be creative which can alleviate some stress	
Excellent for memory since you can visually recall the entire mind map in your head	

Videos, Animations and Slideshows

Visual learners can benefit greatly from watching videos and animations to help them revise. There's a wealth of videos online, often made by people who recently sat exams, which can be used to help you get a better grasp of the material. Head over to a popular video-sharing website such as YouTube and search for the topic you're currently revising. Always double-check that the information that they give is correct and relevant (by comparing what the videos say to what's in your own resources), because it's possible that these people studied for a different test than you.

Watching videos created by people who didn't write your textbooks is great for some subjects because it may offer alternative opinions and viewpoints. This is especially useful for essay-based school subjects such as English Literature, History, and Religious Studies, where having a range of interpretations and different opinions at your disposal can flesh out your answers even further. This is less important for other academic subjects such as the sciences or Maths, but nevertheless these videos still serve their function of being interesting to the eye.

Outside of the usual video-sharing sites, there are plenty of online resources which will give you videos, animations and slideshows to help you get your head around whatever you're currently revising. Again, remember to check that the information you're receiving matches what's in your textbooks.

This method is great for splitting up long sessions of note-taking. If you've spent the whole day revising, and you're getting tired of writing down notes, watching some revision videos online might provide some relief.

> Note: watching videos online can be an excellent way of revising, but make sure that you stay on topic. It's far too easy to get distracted by everything else on the internet (e.g. social media, online games) – stay focused!

Visual Aids: Pros and Cons

Pros	Cons
Can be interesting or even funny to watch, and this can help ideas stick in your brain	Access to the internet can lead to easy distractions if you don't exercise self-restraint
Can give you an insight on alternative arguments and points of view	Sometimes the content in the videos won't completely match what you're being tested on – some things might not be relevant
Works as a good break from more intensive revision activities	

Am I a Visual Learner?

Do you find that you can recall information based on how it's displayed on a page? Try taking some notes or making a mind map based on resources in your textbooks, then turn the paper over and try and re-write the notes. Once you've re-written everything, flip the original page back over and see how well you did at remembering it all. If you could remember most or all of

General Study Techniques 35

it, that probably means that you can learn from visual aids.

Aural Learning

Aural learning is all about listening, both to your own voice and others. Aural learners absorb information by listening to it being said, either by themselves or by others. While it only really involves your ears, aural learning is incredibly flexible. There are plenty of ways to revise effectively if you are an aural learner.

Aural learning is excellent for subjects which have lots of short, sweet bits of information. For example, visual learners will likely write the process down as a series of bullet points, or perhaps a flow chart, whilst aural learners will want to listen to each of these points individually, to allow them to sink in.

Reading Out Loud

This is the simplest method of aural learning, and can be done on your own and without any extra equipment. All you need is yourself, your textbook (or other study materials) and your voice!

Start by opening on a chapter or paragraph that you're comfortable with, and then begin to read it to yourself out loud. When you come across a sentence or point which might be more complicated or confusing, read it multiple times. By doing this, it will stick in your head more, making you more likely to remember it.

Aural learners can benefit from using certain tones

for different points. Singing notes that you need to remember, or creating catchy rhymes for them, can help you to keep them in mind more easily. It might sound silly at first, but they can be incredibly useful.

Aural learners can create acrostics and mnemonics to help them remember difficult spellings or more complex ideas. Acrostics and mnemonics are almost opposites of one another. An acrostic is a phrase you keep in mind to remember lots of smaller phrases or information.

For example, BIDMAS is an acrostic which can be used to remember how you should go about solving maths questions:

Brackets

Indices (or 'powers of')

Division

Multiplication

Addition

Subtraction

Mnemonics, on the other hand, are a collection of words used to remember a single, larger word. These are particularly good for spellings:

BECAUSE = **B**ig **E**lephants **C**an't **A**lways **U**se **S**mall **E**xits

The colours in the rainbow can be remembered using the following mnemonic:

ROYGBIV = **R**ichard **O**f **Y**ork **G**ave **B**attle **I**n **V**ain

You can also use this acrostic to help you remember the colours of the rainbow!

Red

Orange

Yellow

Green

Blue

Indigo

Violet

Aural leaners can repeat the phrase "ROYGBIV" or "Richard of York gave battle in vain" until it sinks in fully. Then, if you got stuck in a test, all you'd need to do is recall the phrase!

Of course, the content at the level you're working at could be much more complicated than "ROYGBIV" or the spelling of "because". However, these exercises can still be used to remember key formulae and phrases.

Note: any kind of learner can make use of acrostics and mnemonics. Even if you aren't an aural learner, try them yourself!

Reading Out Loud: Pros and Cons

Pros	Cons
Requires very little equipment to get started	Requires a specific environment – a place where you're on your own and can speak out loud
Acrostics and other rhymes are bite-sized, meaning you can try remembering them on the go	Can eventually get tiring
Great for making sure you're actually reading the material and taking it in	
Has the potential for self-recording (see below)	

Self-recording

For this technique, all you need is your voice, some reading material and a device which you can record yourself with. In the past, you would have had to use a specific device called a dictation machine to record yourself. Nowadays, almost any modern smartphone or tablet has voice recording capabilities. So long as it has a microphone, it should be able to record your voice as well. If these options aren't available, dictation machines aren't too expensive, and they might be worth the investment.

General Study Techniques

Note: Many laptops can record your voice too. If it has a camera, it's probably capable of recording your voice with its microphone!

If you've chosen to use the "reading aloud" method of revision, you might as well record yourself at the same time. The self-recording technique is quite simple; all you need to do is record yourself reading your notes.

The great thing about this method is that both recording and listening help you to remember information. While you're reading your notes out loud into the microphone, you're going to be committing them to memory, just like you would when reading out loud. Once you're done reading all of them, you can listen to them through speakers or headphones whenever you're studying.

<u>Here are some tips to make your recordings even easier to study from:</u>

- Make sure you're not speaking too close to the microphone, or too far away from it. Do a couple of test runs to make sure your microphone is working properly.

- Speak slowly and clearly, so that you can listen back easily.

- Place emphasis on the more important details in your notes. Try changing your tone of voice for certain key phrases or facts, so that they stick out more.

- When you're done recording, send the files to your phone or smart device so that they're always handy.

Whenever you have a free 10 minutes or so, you can listen to your notes!

Self-recording: Pros and Cons

Pros	Cons
Has all of the benefits of reading out loud	Requires some kind of recording device, might take a while to set up
Allows you to listen back to your recordings later on	

Podcasts and other Recordings

If you don't like hearing your own voice, or don't have a way to record yourself, there are still plenty of resources that you can listen to. Revision podcasts are easily accessible, and quite often free to download and listen to. There are also plenty of resources on YouTube (such as CareerVidz) and other video-sharing websites, which you can listen to via smartphones, computers and tablets.

Remember to make sure that the revision materials are relevant. Depending on the exam board, the topics that you learn may differ. Before listening to a revision podcast, double check that the topics match those in your textbook or syllabus. If you're unsure of where to start, ask your teacher if they know of any resources that may be relevant.

Like self-recording, revision podcasts and other materials

are useful because you can carry them with you at any time, with the help of smartphones and tablets. This means that, wherever you are, you can put a bit of time into listening to them.

Another bonus of these techniques is that they can be far less tiring. Reading out loud from a textbook or writing pages upon pages of notes can get incredibly boring, especially after long sessions. Using revision podcasts can often be a slightly more fun way of learning – so make use of it when you aren't feeling entirely up to more formal revision.

Podcasts and Recordings: Pros and Cons

Pros	Cons
Can be used as a break from doing your own revision	Sometimes exact material in the podcast might not match your curriculum
Can offer alternative ideas and opinions which strengthen your own knowledge	Require some kind of device (e.g. smartphone, tablet, computer or mp3 player) to listen to them
Can be stored on a phone or mp3 player and listened to anywhere	
Often free of charge	

Discussing With Others

Many revision techniques can be quite lonely. Sometimes, it's nice to have a bit of human interaction. Thankfully, aural learners can make use of discussion with a revision partner. This is a great revision method if you have a friend or family member available to help. All this involves is sitting (or standing!) with your revision partner and going through the material with them. There are two different ways in which you could do this:

- **Ask and answer questions.** With this method, your revision partner will hold the textbook in front of themselves for them to read, and then ask questions about the material. It's your job to answer them as accurately as possible. If you get the answer correct, congratulations! Move onto the next one. If you answer incorrectly, your revision partner can steer you in the right direction by revealing a bit more information, such as the first letter of the word, or some related details.

If your revision partner is taking the same test as you, then you should take turns asking and answering questions. By doing this, you're both being exposed to the material and can get things done quickly.

- **Open discussion.** This method involves you and your revision partner speaking freely about the material. If your partner is also studying for an exam, both of you should try to discuss without looking at your textbooks or notes. However, keep the books close by in case both of you can't remember something, or are unsure of precise details. It's also

General Study Techniques

a good idea to share notes too, so that you can make sure that you've got something correct.

If your revision partner isn't studying for the exam (such as a family member), allow them to have the book open in front of them, but so that you can't see it. Then, just speak to them about the things that you're revising, and they can fact-check you along the way.

Both of these methods are great ways to learn with a partner, and are excellent ways of making sure that your other revision techniques are working. Discussing with a partner is most beneficial later on during revision, when you've already learned lots of information by yourself, and just want to test your ability to remember it.

Note: Thanks to modern phones and internet, you don't even need to sit in the same room as your revision partner in order to revise. There are plenty of communication apps and programs that you can download to your phone, tablet or computer which will let you revise with friends.

Discussing with Others: Pros and Cons

Pros	Cons
It's a fantastic way of remembering information, as well as finding out what you know and where you need to improve	Can be difficult to organise, particularly outside of school hours
Benefits two people (you and your revision partner)	It's possible to get distracted and chat about irrelevant things!
It's a great way for friends and family members to get involved in the revision process	

Am I an Aural Learner?

Aural learners tend to focus on what they are hearing and saying more than what they are seeing and doing. If you think this applies to you, give some of the above styles a try. Aural learning is especially useful for those who struggle to sit down and take notes for longer periods of time, and the above techniques can be used by anyone who wants to mix up their revision.

Kinaesthetic Learning

Kinaesthetic learning is all about *doing*, rather than looking or hearing. Kinaesthetic learners shouldn't limit themselves to sitting in one place and trying to write pages full of notes. Instead, they should be finding more creative and unconventional ways of learning. There's a huge range of techniques for a kinaesthetic learner to tap into!

Since kinaesthetic learning is such a broad field, it can apply to almost any subject and any kind of information. If you think you might be a kinaesthetic learner, give some of the following techniques a try.

Flashcards

With flashcards, you'll want to write down some key notes from your textbooks or other revision materials. Take a large piece of card and cut it up into smaller segments. On one side of each card, write down the word or concept that you need to remember the meaning of. On the other, write down the key facts associated with the word. Here's an example to get you started:

Front	Reverse
Sonnet	A fourteen-line poem which is written in iambic pentameter.
	Uses specific rhyme scheme.
	Has a single, focused theme.

Once you've written all of your flashcards, turn them all facing front up and sort them into a deck (like a deck of playing cards). Then, take each card, read out the main word on the front, and then try and recall as many of the key facts as possible. You can do this by reading out loud, or by reading in your head – whichever suits you best.

Once you think you've finished listing them all, flip the card over to see if you missed any details. If you didn't, congratulations! Put the card to one side and save it for later. If you missed anything, take note of it and put the card back at the bottom of the deck. This means that, once you've got through all of the other cards, you can attempt the ones you couldn't completely remember before. One by one, you'll start to eliminate cards from the deck, since you'll remember all of the details for each of them. Once you've completed them all, take a short break before trying again.

Another method for using cards is to stick them around your workspace. Write a note on each piece of card and leave it somewhere in your room where you're likely to see it often. Stick some to your mirror or the edge of a laptop screen, or even place them on the wall or on a bookshelf. You can even leave them around your house so that whenever you stop to make yourself a snack or go to the toilet, you'll still be revising!

Flash Cards: Pros and Cons

Pros	Cons
A pack of small cards is portable, so flashcards can be used wherever you are	Can take a while to put together (writing on individual cards, etc.)
They're incredibly useful for learning key terms and their meanings	
Writing them in the first place helps commit ideas to memory	

Multitasking

Multitasking simply involves doing another activity whilst doing your ordinary revision. By doing this, you'll start to associate certain facts with the things you do. If you enjoy exercise, try listening to recordings of yourself reading out notes, while going for a run or working out in some other way. If you play video games, stop and test yourself on a question every so often. This probably won't work as a main revision technique, but it's a way to do some light revision on a day off, or once you've finished the bulk of your studying for the evening.

Multitasking: Pros and Cons

Pros	Cons
Bite-sized but effective	Doesn't really work as a main revision technique
Can be done anywhere and at any time	
More light-hearted than intense revision sessions	

Learning Games

For this technique, you're probably going to need access to either the internet or dedicated workbooks. You'll want to find games or other interactive tools which involve *doing* things rather than just reading them. For example, one game might require you to match up key words to their meanings, or key dates to the events which occurred on them. You can actually do this one yourself, in the same way that you made flashcards. Cut up a large piece of paper in separate pieces, and then on half of them write a key word. Then write something related to each key word on all of the other pieces. Shuffle up all of the cards, then try to match them up.

You should also check online for other learning games. As always, double check that the content of the games matches that of whatever you're working on, so you don't confuse yourself.

Learning Games: Pros and Cons

Pros	Cons
Entertaining and highly effective for kinaesthetic learners	Online learning games aren't always easy to find
Work as a great break from more intensive revision methods	Creating your own learning games can be time-consuming
Can be an excellent way to revise with others	

Am I a Kinaesthetic Learner?

If you find yourself *doing* things rather than reading or listening, then kinaesthetic learning might be the style for you. You might find that it's much easier for you to do something for yourself, rather than ask someone to explain it to you. You might also find that you work best in unconventional settings: maybe you work better while exercising than sitting at a desk.

Looking Back on Your Earlier Studies

In previous books in this series, we've pointed out that GCSEs and A-Levels are great testing grounds for revision styles and techniques. If you've already studied for exams in the past, you can use this experience to your advantage. While different areas and levels of study will differ greatly in terms of content and difficulty, you can still learn from previous experiences with exams and revision in your life. Consider the following:

- What revision techniques worked best for you in previous exams and assessments? How can you apply them effectively to what you're currently studying?
- What didn't work so well? Is it worth giving it another try?
- What exams went well? Where there any tactics you employed during them that might've helped?
- What exams didn't go so well? What can you learn from your mistakes?

Feel free to experiment with learning styles and revision techniques, but don't be afraid to go back to what suits you best. Sometimes, being in your comfort zone is just what you need in order to perform well.

A Final Word about Learning Styles

The techniques explored here are only a few of the many ways you can learn and revise effectively. Start by experimenting with the methods we've listed, but feel free to branch out and try your own ways of revising. Different people think and work differently to one another, and so you need to find your own unique way of learning that works best for you. Remember that, just because you may believe that you have a specific learning style, you don't have to stick to a limited range of techniques. Be creative and give everything a try – it's the only way to truly know what works best for you.

Additional Learning Styles - Four More Types of Learner

In the last chapter, we looked at the three main learning styles. While it's likely you fall into one or more of those categories, it's possible that none of them really apply to you. In this chapter, we're going to discuss four more learning styles, with a description and tips for each.

Physical Learning

This approach, also known as the 'bodily-kinaesthetic' style, involves using your body and sense of touch to help revise. Physical learners tend to be into activities which make use of the whole body, such as sports, exercise, or gardening. Physical learners like to think about things while they do these activities, and often use them as a way of working through their problems. They also like to go straight into the physical, practical parts of learning as soon as possible. For example, rather than sitting and learning the theory in a Physical Education lesson, physical learners like to do it all for themselves. This style of learning is quite similar to kinaesthetic learning, with the major difference being that physical learners use their bodies more.

Physical learners can take advantage of their sensitivity to the physical world by using gestures and body motions to remember things. For example, if you need to remember a quote for an essay-based exam, you might learn it better by physically acting it out, creating hand and body motions that stick in your brain. Flashcards can also be incredibly useful for physical learners, especially if you move them around a lot or place them around your workspace.

Additional Learning Styles

In addition, physical learners benefit from breathing and relaxation techniques to focus and get in a mindset suitable for revision. Even if you aren't a physical learner, you can probably make use of meditation and relaxation to prepare yourself for revision!

Logical Learning

As the name suggests, logical learners make best use of their brain by engaging in logical and mathematical reasoning. Logical learners are adept at finding patterns in information, and can use them to create mental associations between different facts. In particular, they can easily categorise information, essentially using the 'chunking' method of committing information to memory.

Logical learners tend to work through things in an organised manner. They'll work best under regimented revision schemes, and will likely prefer to categorise everything they need to study. The advantage of this is that they'll get to tick things off as they move through the content. This can be incredibly satisfying. Logical learners might also prefer to place everything in a ranked order.

Logical learners are great at getting 'behind the scenes' of what they're learning. For example, if they have to revise a mathematical formula, they'll perhaps get the urge to figure out *why* the formula is written in a specific way, taking it apart and learning the theory behind it. This is particularly useful for science and maths-based material, but could be applied to any setting.

While logical learners have a lot of advantages when

it comes to revision, they need to avoid getting stuck overanalysing one small detail. They can't get hung up on something that's relatively small in the larger picture of their work. This can take some training, but eventually logical learners can adapt to avoid spending too much time thinking and working on one thing.

Social Learning

Social learners are best suited to communication with others, whether during revision or just in everyday life. Social learners work best in groups or pairs, either discussing their findings directly with one another or collaboratively building revision strategies. Social learners will absolutely benefit from the "discussing with others" method we discussed in the previous chapter, since they'll be able to communicate their own ideas effectively as well as keenly listen to others.

In addition, social learners tend to be good team players. This can be excellent for assessed group exercises, such as presentations, where candidates are tested on how they work with others as well as their individual input.

Social learners should focus on working at least with one other person. Almost any of the methods listed in the previous chapter can be applied to a cooperative setting. A group or pair of learners could make flashcards together, then test each other in a semi-competitive environment. Social learners can also use role-plays to remember events or key concepts, especially if they have a large group of people to work with. Social learners can also get together and create mind maps or do learning games to help them remember the most important facts.

Solitary Learning

The final learning style for this chapter is solitary learning, which is almost the complete opposite of social learning. Solitary learners prefer to study alone, and might find the input of others distracting. Instead, they like to focus on what they think, as opposed to what other people have to say. Revision in a quiet, private space is preferable, or perhaps even necessary.

Since solitary learners work better on their own, they don't have the benefit of talking through ideas and concepts with others. Instead, solitary learners can keep a diary or journal – a space independent of their proper revision notes, where they can write down their own thoughts on a topic.

Combined Learning Styles

As you might've noticed, there's quite a bit of an overlap between these learning styles and those in the last chapter. By all means, mix and match between styles and methods to find what works best for you. In particular, the social/solitary styles work in conjunction with the others, so you might find that you best employ a combination of two or three different styles of learning.

Now that you've had the opportunity to look at 7 different learning styles, we're going to move onto the first, most important step of your revision: getting started!

Getting Started with Your Revision

How To Study: Ace Your Grades

So far, you've had an introduction to different styles of learning, and a detailed look at many revision techniques that can be used in your exams. In this chapter, we'll be shifting the focus slightly, and taking a look at other skills and tricks to help you prepare for any exam. These include:

- How to create a revision timetable;
- How to keep yourself motivated;
- How to prevent yourself from becoming distracted;
- How to avoid cramming;
- How to make use of past papers and mark schemes.

Revision Timetables and Planning

Now that you've had the opportunity to explore the different ways of learning, it's time to turn the focus to other general aspects of revision: creating and sticking to a timetable, and making full use of revision materials. Both are extremely valuable when revising, and proper handling of both will improve your grade and make you more likely to score high in exams and in controlled assessments.

The goal of having a revision timetable is to map out all of the work that needs to be done in time for each exam. Your plan doesn't need to be expertly crafted or even particularly nice to look at; it just needs to be clear and easy to read.

The first thing you should do is list every subject that you

Getting Started with Your Revision

are taking exams in. Once you've done that, try and find every topic or module within that subject. Take a look at the following example, which shows all of the topics an aspiring teacher would have to learn for the punctuation section of the QTS Literacy Skills Test:

- Full stop;
- Comma;
- Paragraphs;
- Colon;
- Semi-colon;
- Question mark;
- Exclamation mark;
- Parentheses (brackets);
- Capital letters;
- Dash;
- Hyphen;
- Speech marks;
- Quotation marks;
- Ellipsis.

You may wish to go into slightly more detail for each of the topics, but as a foundation, this will be enough to fill in a revision timetable. Do this for every module and for every subject, so that you know roughly how much material there is to cover. It's also worth taking a look at how long each of the chapters for these modules are in your textbook, so that you're aware of any abnormally large or small topics.

Once you've done this, it's time to prioritise all of your subjects and topics. Some people like to rank all their subjects from most important to least important. In other words, it might be worth considering which subjects you find more difficult, and giving them higher priority. If you already feel quite confident about a certain part of your studies, place it slightly lower on your list. This means that the areas that need the most attention will receive it.

Once you've prioritised your subjects, you can also prioritise modules. Bear in mind that a lot of topics in many subjects are cumulative – which means that a good understanding of earlier modules is vital for getting to grips with later ones. This is especially the case with Maths and Science, where you're building up knowledge as you go along. For these ones, it's better to start at the beginning and work your way through, but other subjects might allow you to mix things up a bit.

Your timetable should include all of the material that you need to revise outside of school hours. The best way to find out what you need to cover, is to take a look at how your textbooks divide their content, and then use those to fill the timetable. You'll be treated to some blank templates for a timetable at the end of this book.

Getting Started with Your Revision 61

The following example timetable shows what a single week of revision may look like. Take a look at this timetable to get an idea of how to organise your time.

	Monday	Tuesday	Wednesday	Thursday	Friday	Saturday	Sunday
09:00 - 10:00	Work	Work	Work	Work	Work	Grammar Practice	Comprehension Practice
10:00 - 11:00	Work	Work	Work	Work	Work	Grammar Practice	Comprehension Practice
11:00 - 12:00	Work	Work	Work	Work	Work	Grammar Test	Comprehension Test
12:00 - 13:00	Work	Work	Work	Work	Work	Break	Break
13:00 - 14:00	Work	Work	Work	Work	Work	Punctuation Practice	Spelling Practice

14:00 - 15:00	Work	Work	Work	Work	Punctuation Practice	Grammar Practice
15:00 - 16:00	Work	Work	Work	Work	Punctuation Test	Punctuation Practice
16:00 - 17:00	Work	Work	Work	Work	Comprehension Practice	Comprehension Practice
17:00 - 18:00	Break	Break	Break	Break	Comprehension Practice	Comprehension Practice
18:00 - 19:00	Spelling Practice	Grammar Practice	Punctuation Practice	Comprehension Practice	Spelling Practice	Break
19:00 - 20:00	Spelling Practice	Grammar Practice	Punctuation Practice	Comprehension Practice	Spelling Test	Break

If you're still at school (perhaps studying for your GCSEs or A-Levels) then make sure to factor in the school day. If you're working full-time, make sure you take this into account too. If you are working every day of the week, it might be worth leaving the bulk of your revision to the weekend, because you might be too tired on a weeknight. Figure out what works best for you before creating your full revision timetable.

If you are at school, then be sure to make full use of the holidays. These are perfect for getting whole days of revision under your belt, since you won't be at school. All of a sudden you don't have to go to school for 6 hours a day, meaning that you have a lot more time on your hands. While you may want to take a break from everything, you should make use of all the free time you have during these breaks. In fact, many students do the bulk of their revision during these holidays. Of course, you should take some time off, but make sure you take advantage of the holiday period. This can really put you ahead for the next school term.

How Do I Motivate Myself?

Getting motivated to revise in the first place can be incredibly difficult, and requires a lot of determination and self-control. The earlier you start your revision, the better, but you'll probably be tempted to put off revision: "I'll start next week", or "it's way too early to start revising." Try and start revising 8 weeks before your first exam. This should give you plenty of time to get through all of your topics.

Getting Started with Your Revision 65

However, even starting the process can be a pain, and when the exams are so far away it's difficult to get the ball rolling. So, you need to motivate yourself to start revising as early and as well as possible. In this section, we'll take a look at some of the ways you can keep yourself motivated and make sure you get through your revision.

Revision Styles

Start by finding revision styles that you actually enjoy. This might sound ridiculous, but if you can find a few techniques that aren't completely unbearable, you'll be more willing to make a start with revision. Remember that you don't have to be constantly doing 'hard revision' such as note-taking. Mix things up and try a number of styles to keep things fresh early on, then maybe move into something more serious later.

Ease Into It

Before you start, revision can feel like a huge mountain, impossible to climb to the top of. It can be incredibly daunting. You might be overwhelmed by the feeling that you are completely unprepared and don't know enough. That said, you need to make a start sometime. Some revision is better than no revision at all, so if you're struggling to get started with your studies, ease your way into it. Start by revising for a much shorter period of time, and maybe focus on the things that you already know well or most enjoy. Once you're comfortable and confident, move onto something that you're less sure of.

Treat Yourself

Make sure you keep yourself motivated with some treats. You don't need to go overboard, but the "carrot and stick" method of revision can keep you working for longer periods of time, allowing you to get through more work. Things like "I'll get some ice cream, but only after I've done the next 3 pages" are a great way of keeping you going and keeping your spirits up.

Think Ahead

Finally, always think ahead past exams. Life continues after your exams. You might feel that you're not in a great place while revising, that your social life is suffering or your free time is being eaten up by studies, but it will all be worth it when you get great results. This positive outlook – thinking towards the future – is one of the best ways to get you started with revision, and keep you going with it too.

Staying Focused

Sometimes, revision can be a total pain, and you'd rather do anything (even sit around doing absolutely nothing!) than open a book and do some hard learning. It's very tempting to procrastinate, but falling into the trap of putting off revision is one of the biggest mistakes you can possibly do.

Getting Started with Your Revision

Here are our top 5 tips for avoiding procrastination and getting on with your work!

Turn Off Distractions

The first thing you should do before starting a revision session is remove any distractions from your workspace. The biggest offenders are often games consoles, social media, mobile phones, and of course television. The simple solution to this is to turn off these devices, and put them somewhere out of view or reach, so you aren't tempted to turn them back on and continue texting, messaging or playing games.

Sometimes, however, it isn't practical to move all of these devices. In this case, it's better to find a new workspace, free of electronic devices and other distractions. Many people find that their kitchen or dining room table is an excellent place to study, but find what works best for you and your home. If there's nowhere in your house that's suitable for studying, the local library may be a good choice.

When choosing a place to study, consider the following:

- Is it quiet?
- Are there any gadgets to distract you?
- Will people be walking in and out of the room? Will that distract you?
- Is it comfortable?
- Is there plenty of room for you and all of your notes?

Things get a little trickier when you're using computerised or other online resources such as revision games or podcasts. In these cases, you're going to need your computer, phone or tablet with you, so you'll need to exercise some self-control. Log yourself out of social media if you feel that it's necessary to do so, and make sure to turn off notifications for messaging apps on your phone. You can always take a look during your breaks.

Finally, a few words about listening to music while revising. Be very careful when playing music (especially music with lyrics) while studying. It works for some people, but others will find it incredibly distracting. Experiment with it for yourself, but if you find that it doesn't help you, promptly turn it off.

Give Yourself Plenty of Breaks (but not too many!)

Believe it or not, one of the best ways to avoid procrastination is to take regular breaks. Concentration levels will slide as hours pass, so don't push yourself to revise for too long. If you do this, you'll likely get distracted by almost everything around you, or just get bored or tired. The solution to this problem is to place regular breaks after every chunk of time spent revising. So, if you revise for 45 minutes, you should give yourself a 10 or 15-minute break afterwards. Start with this and then adjust it as necessary, until you get into a routine which is comfortable for you. Remember not to go overboard with breaks. Make sure that you stick to your timetable and routine, so that a 15-minute break doesn't turn into an hour spent watching TV!

Stick to Your Revision Timetable

Writing and filling in a revision timetable is one thing, but it's another thing entirely to stick to it throughout your entire exam season. If it helps, make your timetable more detailed to include breaks and other activities.

It can be tempting to put off revision or bargain with yourself: "I'll only do 2 hours today but I'll make up for it tomorrow," or "I don't really need to know this stuff, I'll take the rest of the day off." Both of these are risky mind-sets, which don't put you in a great place for succeeding. Good organisation skills come in handy here, and you should try and keep to your timetable as much as possible.

Of course, you can be flexible with your time. Sometimes things come up, and you shouldn't completely sacrifice your social life during the revision period. Just make sure it's reasonable, though.

Make Your Working Environment Comfortable

Outside of keeping things quiet and free from distracting gadgets, you should make sure that your revision space is comfortable enough for you to work in. If the room is too cold or hot, or your chair isn't comfortable to sit on, then you might find yourself not wanting to revise. Make sure your revision space is as comfortable as possible.

Mix Things Up

The final tip for staying focused is to mix things up every so often. One way to do this, is to change the subject that you're revising halfway through the day. This means that you'll still be revising, and you'll keep things fresh. You don't need to switch it up too often, but when you find yourself getting too bored of a topic to continue, finish it and then move onto something else entirely, preferably an area from another subject.

You could also change your revision techniques from time to time, to keep things interesting. If you've spent the whole morning writing notes, why not switch over to a podcast or some learning games? You can refer back to our section on different learning styles to get some ideas on how to make your revision more varied.

Cramming and Why You Should Avoid It

Cramming is the act of trying to stuff in as much revision as possible in the days (or even hours!) just before the exam. It's also possibly the biggest act of sabotage that you can do to yourself.

Cramming happens when a candidate either does very little or no revision before the exams. Before they know it, the exam dates have crept up on them, sending them into a state of panic. These candidates tend to then rush through their textbooks and materials, trying to cover weeks' worth of work in just a few days. In almost every case, this is simply not enough time to adequately revise everything. So, people who cram very rarely benefit from it.

Cramming can actually worsen your performance in an exam. Students who cram often find themselves completely blanking on information when they start

Getting Started with Your Revision

answering questions, leaving them helpless during an exam. Cramming doesn't work because you aren't giving your brain enough time to let information sink in.

In an ideal world, you should try to finish your revision for a subject 2 or 3 days before the exam starts. This doesn't always go to plan, but aim to have your revision finished at least 2 days before. Revising the night before an exam is a bad idea, and you should avoid doing so. The day before your exam (and in the hours leading up to it as well) should be spent relaxing and keeping calm, eating well and not allowing yourself to become stressed out by looming thoughts about the test. If you get to the day before your exam and you've finished everything, then you've done an excellent job, and deserve an evening to relax.

Using Mock Exams and Practice Questions

Once you're well into your revision, you'll find that you've got lots of information swimming around in your head. When you feel like you're getting to this point, it may be time to attempt a mock exam. These are excellent ways of testing how much you already know, and it also gives you an insight into what you still need to do in order to ace your exams.

Mock exams are so useful that some people use them and no other techniques when revising. This isn't strictly advised – it's better that you start by revising your notes before trying a mock test, mainly because you may not know enough or remember enough to fully complete a mock exam.

How Do I Find Mock Exams?

This will depend on what you're studying for, whether its school, university, or employment-based exams.

Teachers and Instructors

Finding mock exams is usually quite easy. The first port of call is your teacher, or some other kind of academic advisor. It's possible that they have some mock exams already printed to give to you. If they don't, then it might be worth suggesting that they make some available for yourself and other students.

If your teacher doesn't have any mock exams prepared, try and find out as much about the exam(s) you want to revise for before looking up papers. You need to find out the following before looking up past papers:

- Your exam board – you'll probably need to go to their website to find accurate past papers;

- The name of your specification – sometimes there are 'A' and 'B' versions of the same subject, offered as separate courses (e.g. "Biology A" and "Biology B");

- The year that you'll be sitting your exams – specifications tend to change every few years and that means some older past papers might be irrelevant.

The easiest resources to access are past papers, or actual exams from previous years. These are free to download from exam board websites and can be read

Getting Started with Your Revision 73

from your computer screen, or printed off so that you can write on them.

In addition, there are plenty of workbooks specific to your subjects, which will include practice papers and sample questions.

Printing pages upon pages of past papers can get expensive, but it can be a vital way to learn where your strengths lie and where you need to improve. A solution which will allow you to take advantage of mock papers, as well as save you money on printer ink, is to find settings on your printer such as 'draft' or 'ink saver' mode. These will print the past papers out in a slightly lower quality, but usually the papers are still entirely useable.

Job Applications and Qualifications

If you're applying for a job, this can be a bit more difficult. A lot of careers require you to complete some kind of exam or assessment as part of the application process, and these can be so varied that it's hard to find good sources of information on them. In some cases, you'll be able to find online practice tests and exercises. However, there are plenty of books that offer sample questions for you to read and learn with. Head to www.how2become.com to get free practice tests, as well as find books which cover what you're preparing for.

In the current age, a lot of assessments in the application process are taken on a computer. Tests such as e-tray exercises are entirely interactive, which means the assessment will be computer-based. Practice tests for these kinds of exercises can be found online. The advantage of these practice exercises is that they usually come with a time limit, so you have to complete it in the same time that you would in the real thing. This means that you'll be forced to sit the practice exercises under timed conditions!

How Should I Use Mock Exams?

There are two different ways to use mock exams in your revision. The first way is to attempt a full mock exam as you work through topics of the subject. For example, say that you have a Science exam with three different sections. One of these sections is on evolution and adaptation, the next is on the human anatomy, and the final section is about how drugs and other substances can have an effect on the body. You figure out that these are the three topics you need to learn, so you go through past papers online, focusing on questions revolving around these three topics.

Alternatively, you can work through every topic for the exam, and then move onto past papers. The advantage of this method means that you can spend a chunk of time focusing completely on taking notes and using other revision techniques, then move onto working through whole mock papers. This means that you can simulate the experience of being in an actual exam.

Simulating Exam Conditions

Mock papers and past papers are really useful because they allow you to sit a test as if it was the real thing. To do this, find out how much time you would be given to finish the paper in an actual exam – this information can usually be found on the front of the past paper. Then, gather your pens, pencils and other tools, put your notes aside and find a quiet place. Then, get to work with the mock test.

Time yourself with a clock or stopwatch (most mobile phones come equipped with a stopwatch), and see how long it takes you to complete the paper. What's even more useful is to time how long each section, or even each question, takes you to complete. So, if you find yourself running short on time, you know exactly which topics or types of question need greater focus. You don't want to try and speed through your paper too quickly, but if you're taking an unusually long amount of time on shorter questions, then you know that you need to improve on them.

The best part of using mock exams and past papers is that you can put yourself to the test, and make sure of two things. Firstly, you can make sure that you can recall the material you'll need to remember in the real exam. This comes into effect when you simulate a real exam environment, by doing the test under timed conditions and without your notes. While you're doing the mock tests, you'll probably get an idea of what you can and can't recall. Whenever you can't remember the answer to a question, or there's a key fact you can't recall, make a note on a spare sheet of paper, or at the side of your answer booklet. Then, once you finish the paper, you know exactly what you need to go back to and revise some more.

Mock tests are also useful because they highlight things that you thought you knew, but perhaps didn't get entirely correct. This will become clear when you take a look at the mark scheme, which we will cover in more detail later on in this chapter.

After the Past Papers…

Once you're finished with the mock paper, look at the mark scheme and see how well you did. For school subjects with clear "right or wrong" answers, such as Maths or the sciences, this is quite easy – all you need to do is read the answer then see if it matches what you wrote. For essay-based subjects such as English, this is trickier since the answers you give aren't necessarily right or wrong. In these exams, you tend to be judged on how well you write rather than what you write exactly. In this case, you might need to ask an instructor.

If you're at school, ask your teacher to take a look at your past papers, and they might be able to take a quick look at it. If they have the time, they might go ahead and mark it properly, giving you an idea of where you've done well and where you need to improve. If possible, get a full breakdown of marks so you know exactly what aspects of your exam you need to focus on.

If you're preparing for entrance exams for a job, it can be harder to find someone to mark your work. However, online practice tests tend to show your marks upon completion, and sometimes show an exact breakdown of where you scored well and where you need to improve.

In the next section, we'll examine a mark scheme in more

detail. You'll learn how they work, and more importantly how to use them to make your revision more focused. For now, feast your eyes on the flowcharts. These show two different ways of including mock tests in your revision strategy.

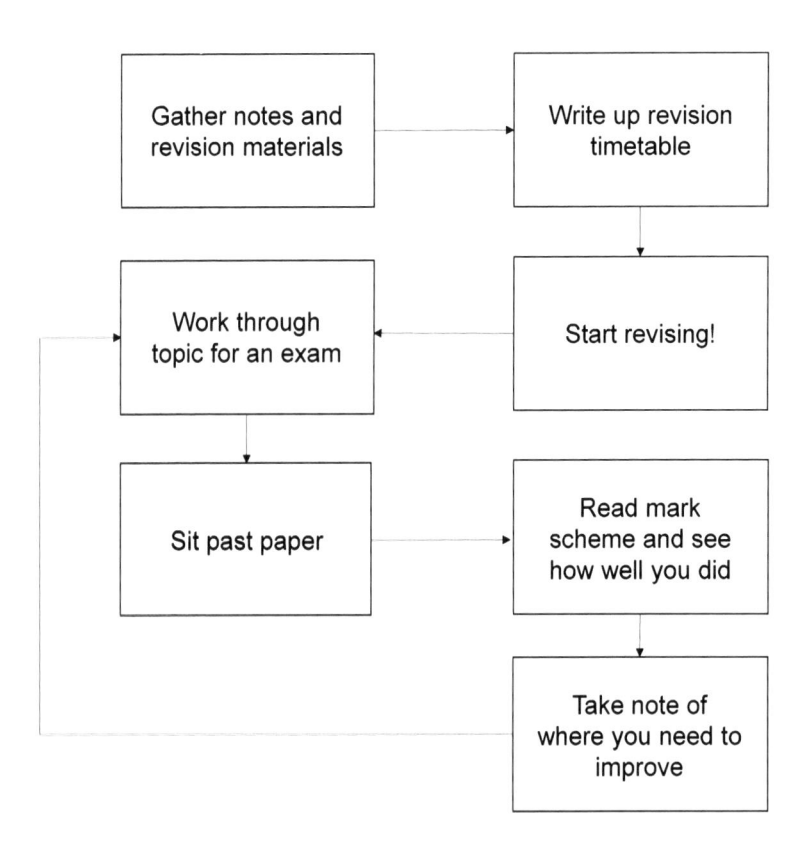

```
Gather notes and          →   Write up revision
revision materials            timetable
                                    ↓
Work through              ←   Start revising!
topic for an exam
      ↓
Sit past paper            →   Read mark
                              scheme and see
                              how well you did
                                    ↓
                              Take note of
                              where you need to
                              improve
```

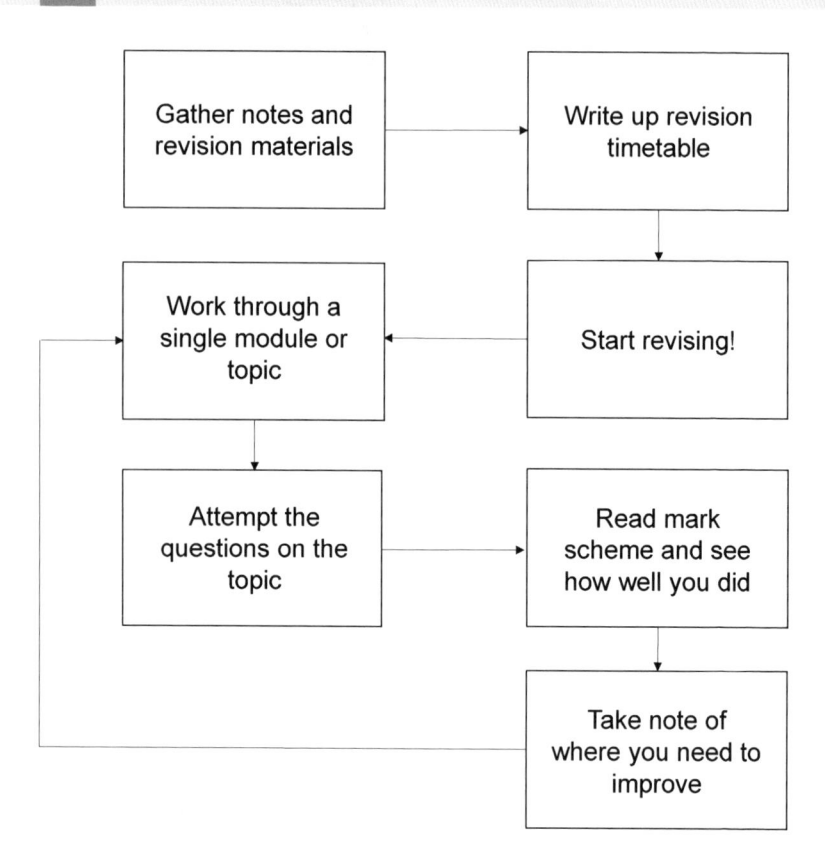

```
┌─────────────────────┐      ┌─────────────────────┐
│  Gather notes and   │ ───▶ │  Write up revision  │
│  revision materials │      │      timetable      │
└─────────────────────┘      └─────────────────────┘
                                        │
                                        ▼
┌─────────────────────┐      ┌─────────────────────┐
│   Work through a    │ ◀──  │   Start revising!   │
│  single module or   │      │                     │
│        topic        │      │                     │
└─────────────────────┘      └─────────────────────┘
           │
           ▼
┌─────────────────────┐      ┌─────────────────────┐
│    Attempt the      │ ───▶ │    Read mark        │
│   questions on the  │      │  scheme and see     │
│        topic        │      │   how well you did  │
└─────────────────────┘      └─────────────────────┘
                                        │
                                        ▼
                             ┌─────────────────────┐
                             │    Take note of     │
                             │  where you need to  │
                             │       improve       │
                             └─────────────────────┘
```

Mark Schemes

Once you've done some practice papers, you'll want to know how well you've done. As we've mentioned previously, mock papers show you what you need to remember, what you know and what you need to improve on. However, sitting the paper is only half of the story. You'll also need to use a mark scheme to figure out what you do and don't know.

What Are Mark Schemes?

Mark schemes are papers which examiners use when marking your exam. In the case of past papers, the mark schemes are the same ones which official examiners would use to mark your exams. So, they're the most accurate source for answers. Depending on the exam, a mark scheme will include different content. For example, Science exams will often simply give the correct answers since the questions are either right or wrong.

However, marking any form of essay response isn't as straightforward. That said, the examiner will have specific marking criteria, which they will use to figure out what the quality of your work is. This is reflected in the mark scheme with a detailed description of what a higher-level essay will look like, and will compare it to other essays of all quality levels. This can make it difficult to mark your own essays, so having your teacher mark them is very useful.

Mark schemes and answer sections can usually be found in the same place where you downloaded the practice papers. Keep away from looking at the mark schemes until you've finished the papers – you don't want to spoil the tests – but have them ready to go.

> **Note:** with a few exceptions, the contents of these sections on mark schemes and examiners' reports won't be relevant to those studying for tests as part of a job application. If you're applying for jobs and taking tests as part of that, head down to our section called 'Asking For Feedback', since this will be more relevant to you. However, if you're studying for GCSE, A-Level, or university exams, the following sections are worth your attention.

What are the Benefits of Using Mark Schemes?

Exam Criteria – Essays

Mark schemes have uses beyond simply finding out whether you have the answers right or wrong. In fact, reading mark schemes can be useful even if you aren't sitting a past paper, because they'll show you what type of answers that the examiners are looking for. This is especially the case in essay-based exams, such as English, as well as other exams which include essays, such as Modern Foreign Languages, History and Geography. You can use mark schemes to find out what criteria the examiners use to mark your exams, and then compare what you've written to see how well you've done. Have you mentioned the key information that's listed for each answer? Have you answered the questions clearly, using an appropriate structure? Have you checked your spelling? All of these are going to be picked up on in essay-based exams, but it's worth reading a mark scheme to see how much each of these aspects affect your grade.

Jumping Through Hoops and Keywords

The other useful aspect of mark schemes is that they'll reveal key phrases and terms, and this is vital for students studying for their A-Levels, GCSEs, or any other kind of academic exam. At GCSE, you're often being tested on sheer knowledge and your ability to recall information. This means that knowing the key words is extremely important at GCSE level, and you can often net marks simply by dropping the key words into your answer.

However, this changes at A-Level. While knowing key terms is still important, in many subjects you're being assessed on *understanding* rather than regurgitation of key facts. This means that, while key terms are important, you won't automatically earn marks just by mentioning them. Quite often, they have to have some kind of explanation, or application to a scenario. This is the essence of the jump from GCSE to A-Level.

At degree level, simply knowing keywords becomes less relevant for a lot of subjects, since questions tend to become more open-ended, and you're being judged on understanding even further. This will depend on the subject that you choose to study.

With all this said, knowing key terms will still be important for succeeding in certain university subjects. For example, you will often need to remember key words and use them as foundations for your writing – either by basing your ideas upon them or arguing that other elements of the issue are more important. All in all, being aware of key facts/quotes/dates will still be required to win marks!

Exact Breakdown of Marks

Mark schemes can also be used to get an exact breakdown of an answer. Using the same example, the answer may award a single mark for lots of different things. For example, a question in a Biology paper could look like the following:

> *How does an asthma attack reduce airflow?*

One answer given could be:

> *When an asthma attack occurs, airflow is reduced because the following three things happen. Firstly, the muscle walls of the bronchioles tighten and contract, leading to a narrower space. Secondly, more mucus is produced by the bronchioles. Combined, this results in the diameter of the airways decreasing in size. This results in airflow being reduced.*

For this example, let's assume two things. Firstly, let's accept this as an entirely correct answer – it got full marks. Also, let's say that this answer is worth three marks. The mark scheme may distribute the marks as follows:

> *1 mark for mentioning each of the following:*
> - *Muscle walls of bronchioles contract/tighten;*
> - *The bronchioles produce more mucus;*
> - *Diameter of the airways are reduced.*

Now that we know what got us the marks, we can highlight them in the answer written.

Getting Started with Your Revision

> *When an asthma attack occurs, airflow is reduced because the following three things happen. Firstly, the <u>muscle walls of the bronchioles tighten and contract</u>, leading to a narrower space. Secondly, <u>more mucus is produced by the bronchioles</u>. Combined, this results in <u>the diameter of the airways decreasing in size.</u> This results in airflow being reduced.*

So, the breakdown of marks tells you exactly what you need to include in your answer, which will give you an idea of what you need to remember for the exam. Bear in mind that you might need to know more than what's given in the mark schemes, since you could be faced with a question which tackles the same topic but from a slightly different angle.

This information in the mark scheme means you could focus your answer even more. You might notice that a lot of the example answer is not underlined, and these details might not be necessary in order to gain full marks. With the information in the mark scheme, we can simplify and focus our answer:

> *Firstly, the <u>muscle walls of the bronchioles contract</u>. <u>More mucus is produced by the bronchioles</u>. Both of these <u>reduce the diameter of the airways</u>. This results in reduction in airflow.*

Now this answer is much shorter, but should earn you the same amount of marks. So, we now have a much shorter answer, which will give us as many marks as the longer answer would. This saves time, allowing us to move onto other questions in the exam.

'Waffling' is what people tend to do when they aren't sure how to answer a question. Students who waffle in an exam will add lots of extra words to their answers to fill them out, even if none of what they are saying will earn them marks. We'll discuss waffling in more detail in the next chapter, but remember that reading a mark scheme and finding out exactly what earns you points should help you to avoid writing meaningless rubbish!

Giving Precise Answers

In an exam, you might be tempted to fire off everything you know about a topic all at once. While it's great that you've remembered lots of information, it's not always a good idea to write absolutely everything you know when answering a question. Instead, you should figure out exactly what the question is asking from you. In the above example, we included a lot of information that wasn't necessary to get full marks.

You should aim to be as precise as possible with your answer – get straight to the point in order to save time. Mark schemes are useful here, because they'll show you what the examiners are looking for. You can figure out what's required to get full marks in a question, then focus on giving that as your answer. In an exam, every second is precious; the less time you spend on unnecessary information, the more time you have for harder questions or for double-checking your work at the end. Efficiency is a great skill to have when it comes to exams, and using mark schemes to hone your answers will help you to achieve this.

As well as saving you time, working on giving precise

answers can make you sound more confident when giving your answers. Too much information can come across as waffle.

With all this said, it's important that you make sure you answer every question in an exam as fully as possible. If you aren't sure what to write in your answer, it's better to give more information than less.

Examiners' Reports

The final pieces of documentation you can get from an exam board are called "examiners' reports". These are documents written by chief examiners at an exam board, drawing from exam results and mark breakdowns from previous years, to take note of what students as a whole did well, and where they need to improve. These can be useful for looking into larger questions, such as long essays, and finding out which areas students tend to fall down on. Then, you can compare this to how comfortable you are with the same elements, and in turn work a bit more on them if necessary. You can find these on exam board websites.

Asking For Feedback

When applying for any role, there's always the possibility that you won't be accepted. While this can be irritating, especially when you've spent hours preparing for tests and interviews, it isn't the end of the world. Instead, you should try and get some feedback from the employers. Occasionally, test results will be emailed to you immediately after completing them, or at the point where you've been rejected during the application process. If this doesn't happen, get the email address of the recruiters and politely ask for some feedback on anything that you did for them. It may just be a case of showing you what you got right and wrong in a maths test, or it might go deeper, giving detailed accounts of your answers, and where you need to improve. Not all employers will offer feedback, but it's definitely worth getting some from ones who supply it.

Conclusion

So, by this point you hopefully have the following: a revision timetable, a comfortable space to work, an idea of what your learning style is, and some ideas to get you started with revision. You've also been given some ideas about how to make use of both mock papers and mark schemes to increase your grade. You're now well on your way to taking your exams and succeeding.

Next, we'll be looking at exams: what they are, how to deal with revising for them, and how to perform well in them!

Exam Techniques and Preparation

Exams can be difficult, and you need to prepare for them in two different ways. First, you need to know the content of the exam. This is the actual information that you are going to be tested on – the stuff you've been learning in class, or on your course.

The second thing you need to learn is how to answer exam questions, and how to perform well in exams. This might sound strange, but a significant part of doing well in exams comes down to your familiarity with them, not just how well you know your subjects.

In a later chapter, we'll discuss subject-specific tips for exams. For now, take a look at these general tips, which will help you in the days before and during your exams.

Practise Handwriting Beforehand

If your exams are handwritten, you need to make sure that your handwriting is legible. In the exam room, people tend to write incredibly quickly. As the exam goes on, some students will write more frantically, while others might slowly ease into the exam and get better as time goes on. Either way, ensure that your handwriting is as easy to read as possible.

If the examiner can't read what you've written, they won't be able to mark your work. Generally speaking, it's only the most severe handwriting that results in a significant loss of marks, but if you know that your handwriting isn't as good as it could be, it's worth taking some time to practise it. If possible, try and incorporate handwriting practice into your revision so that you save time. Dedicated handwriting time is good, but you may as well kill two birds with one stone and use revision techniques that help your handwriting, such as making flashcards or writing out pages of notes. If you've been doing mock papers under timed conditions, this should have helped as well.

In the exam, make sure to take your time if you feel as though your handwriting is suffering. If it helps, ditch cursive (joined-up) handwriting so that the words are easier to read.

Finally, you want to practise handwriting so that your muscles are used to writing for extended periods of time. This is important for avoiding hand cramp. Find a way of gripping the pen which is as comfortable as possible, whilst also being able to write efficiently and neatly. Learning some exercises to gently warm up your hands before the exam can also be helpful, and will hopefully make you less worried about your hands giving up halfway through.

If your assessments are based on the computer, you obviously don't need to worry about handwriting. However, if you need to type out your answers, take some time to work on your typing so that you can answer questions quickly and with no typing errors. Being able to touch-type is preferable, but not necessary – just make sure that you can type at a decent pace and with a high level of accuracy.

How To Study: Ace Your Grades

Come Prepared

Always make sure that you have all of the equipment necessary for completing an exam. This will depend on the subject and the module, so find out beforehand what you're allowed to take in with you.

The following are things that you can take into almost any exam:

- **Black pens.** You should always take a few black ballpoint pens into your exams. Generally speaking, blue pens are not allowed, neither are fountain-pens, since the ink can run more easily on them. Ballpoints are the standard for most exam boards.

- **Pencils.** You might not need these for every exam, but it's worth bringing them for rough planning, just in case.

- **Clear pencil case.** Again, this might not be necessary, but bringing a pencil case can help you be more organised. Make sure it's clear though – if the exam invigilators can't see into the pencil case easily, they may confiscate it because you could be using it to hide notes and cheat!

- **Bottle of water.** We'll talk more about this later on, but bringing a bottle of water can help you concentrate – you don't want to get dehydrated. Remember to make sure that the bottle is clear and has no labels.

Exam Techniques and Preparation

Depending on the exam, other pieces of equipment may be appropriate, such as:

- **Calculator.** Certain Maths and Science exams will allow you to bring calculators. Other exams in these subjects might not allow for calculators. If you aren't sure, bring it with you anyway and then leave it under your desk, and hand it to an invigilator if it isn't allowed.

- **Rulers and protractors.** Equipment for solving angles may be allowed for some exams. Like calculators, however, they won't be allowed for others. Make sure that they are transparent (clear).

- **Books.** Be careful with this one. Some exams might allow you to bring in a specific book, such as some English or language exams at school. Others will be referred to as 'closed-book' exams, which means you can't take in any notes or materials – including the books that you've studied.

If you aren't sure which equipment you're allowed to bring into the exam, ask well in advance.

Keep Calm

Getting a handle on your nerves can be really difficult during exam season, but remember that this is completely normal. If you consider that doing well in your exams is very important, then it would be bizarre for you not to be at least a bit nervous. Millions of people will be going through the same thing as you, and millions more have been in your position and have made it out of the other end in one piece. Life goes on after your exam, even if it doesn't feel like that during the heat of the moment.

Exams are stressful, and the conditions you take them in aren't pleasant either. Being stuck in a silent room for an hour, with nothing but a question paper and your own thoughts, can be incredibly daunting. However, you need to remember that you're not the only one who feels this way, and that a bit of nerves can give you the boost you need in the exam hall.

That being said, you need to keep any anxiety under control. A breakdown just before the exam (or even worse, during it) is uncommon, but just remember that not doing as well as you'd hoped in a single exam isn't the end of the world.

You might feel as though you aren't prepared enough, or perhaps a classmate or colleague has made you unsure about what you've revised – minutes before entering the exam room. This happens often, and can be incredibly demoralising. Remember that how prepared you think you are doesn't necessarily represent how well prepared you actually are. Sometimes, people who feel poorly prepared for some exams in the minutes before taking it end up doing incredibly well, and some people find themselves doing worse in exams that they felt completely ready for. Essentially, you never truly know how prepared you are.

Besides, what's the use in worrying on the day of the exam? There's no time left to go back and revise some more, so there's no point in getting stressed about it once you're in the room. Try and get into the current

Exam Techniques and Preparation 93

moment and power through it.

If you're a student at AS level, remember that you've still got the next year to make up for things if you don't do as well as expected. A2 is usually worth more in terms of marks than AS level, so you can certainly make up for it the following year.

Here are some other tips for keeping calm in the exam:

- **Breathing exercises.** If you find yourself getting nervous before exams, or struggle to get to sleep due to exam anxiety, then breathing exercises could be beneficial.

- **Get into the moment.** Just before and during your exam, it can help to go into "exam-mode". By this, we mean blocking off outside distractions and any negativity coming from anywhere. Sometimes, having friends and classmates talk about the possible contents of the exam just before entering can put you off. It might make you feel as if you've missed out on something major, and then cause you to worry once you enter the exam room. Put all of this out of your mind as soon as you enter the room. Once you're in the exam, there's no use fretting about those details.

- **Positive thinking**. This might seem obvious, but thinking positively about the exam and what comes after can be extremely helpful. Some people like to change their mind-set about exams, thinking of it as an opportunity to show off their knowledge, rather than as a painful task that they have to work their way through. Alternatively, focus on what you **do** know rather than what you **don't** know, what you **can** do rather than what you **can't** do. Once you're in the exam room, there's no point worrying about your weaknesses. Focus on your strengths.

Read Instructions Carefully

This sounds simple, but far too many people trip up on this simple bit of advice. When you enter your exam, the first thing you should do is read the instructions on the front of the question or answer paper. In some cases, an invigilator may read the instructions to you, but feel free to read the instructions before the exam starts.

Keep an eye out for instructions on what questions to answer. In some exams, you'll have a choice of which questions you answer, rather than having to answer every question. In these cases, you need to make sure that you know exactly what's required of you, so that you don't waste time answering questions that you don't need to answer. The only thing worse than finding out at the end of the exam that you answered questions unnecessarily, is realising that you didn't answer enough of them!

When you are given a choice of two or more questions to answer (especially in essay subjects), make sure you clearly show which questions you are answering. In some exams, you'll have to tick a box to show what question you're attempting, whilst others will require you to write the question number in your answer section. Either way, keep an eye on the instructions before going ahead and starting the question. This will prevent you from wasting time answering questions that you don't need to attempt, and also stop you from accidentally missing questions that need answering.

Answer the Easiest Questions First

This tip is absolutely key for the tougher exams you come across, since it's an excellent way to use your time in the exam hall effectively.

Say you're about to sit an exam. You sit down and have the examination instructions read out to you. The invigilator instructs you to start your exam, and then you begin. You open the question booklet to find that the first question seems almost impossible. Before you panic, take a flick through the booklet and take a look at some of the other questions. If possible, pick the question that looks the easiest to you and start with that.

This is a good technique for two reasons. Firstly, it's a great boost to your confidence when you're feeling unsure about the exam. There's not much worse in an exam than sitting there, becoming more and more demoralised by a question that you don't think you can answer. Starting with more manageable questions will help you ease into the exam, and hopefully you'll recall some information while doing it.

Sometimes, exams can fit together like a puzzle. At first, it seems impossible. But, once you start to put pieces in (answer the questions), the more difficult bits start to make sense. All of a sudden, you're on a roll of answering questions, and then the tough ones don't seem so bad!

The other reason that this is a good technique, is that it represents a good use of your time. There's no point sitting and staring blankly at a question that you can't solve, when there are others that you could be getting on with. Forget about the tough questions for now, bank as many marks as you can with the easier ones, then go back to the hard ones at the end if you have time. This way, you can secure as many marks as possible. In the worst-case scenario, you won't be able to complete the tough questions, but you'll still have earned a few points for all of the others.

Answer the Question

One of the biggest mistakes that students make throughout their academic lives is failing to answer the question that they've actually been asked. This is particularly the case for essay-based exams such as English Literature, but applies to all of your exams.

Focus on Key Details

Some candidates have a tendency to read a question briefly, then jump straight into their answer without thinking about what's really being asked. For questions which are worth lots of marks, you should take extra care in reading the question fully. If it helps, underline the key parts of the question, so that it's easier to break down:

What were the main causes of the First World War?

Exam Techniques and Preparation

This becomes:

> What were the *main causes* of the *First World War*?

We can figure out a few things from underlining the key points in this question. Firstly, we know that the topic of the question is the First World War. In particular, we need to be looking at the causes of the war. So, our answer is going to be focused on the time period leading up to the start of the First World War in 1914.

However, there's more to the question than this. This question specifies the "main" causes of the First World War. So, we don't need to talk about every single cause of the war, just a few of the most important or biggest things which caused the First World War to happen, such as the assassination of Archduke Franz Ferdinand and rising tensions between the European empires.

<u>Already, we've figured out that we need to answer the question in the following way:</u>

- You need to talk about the causes of the First World War (events up to 1914).

- You need to limit your answer to the main (biggest) causes of the war.

Highlighting the key points of the question has proven useful, because it's pointed out exactly what the question is asking of us. This means that we can save time by answering exactly what we need to, rather than talking about things that won't get us any extra marks.

Don't Twist the Question

Sometimes, students see a question that they don't particularly like the look of. Perhaps it's for a topic that they've studied well and enjoyed, but the question takes a slightly different direction to one that they're used to. For example, a student may have studied the Shakespeare play *Othello* as part of English Literature, and really liked the dastardly villain, Iago. In the exam, they might come across a question on the play, but not specifically about Iago. The question could be:

> *How does Shakespeare show the relationship between Othello and his wife, Desdemona?*

This question is primarily focused on the main character, Othello, and his wife, Desdemona. While the character of Iago plays into most elements of *Othello*, it might be tricky to include him in a discussion about the relationship between Othello and Desdemona. So, you'd need to avoid straying from the topic of the question, even if there's something you would rather write about. Twisting the question into something that you want to answer is a trap that quite a lot of exam-takers fall into, and this ends up costing them marks – particularly in essay subjects. Writing a short plan for your answer, and reading the question carefully, can help you avoid this.

Double-Check the Question

In the next section, we'll be talking about double-checking answers, but it's just as important to double-check the question that you're answering, before you begin to answer it. Say you're doing a maths question:

Exam Techniques and Preparation

> $8.93 \times 9.54 = ?$

Before you start answering the question, take note of everything about it. Where are the decimal points? What operation needs to be performed? Sometimes, people make silly mistakes and misread the question, getting things mixed up.

It's not pleasant finding out that you've answered a question incorrectly just as you get to the end of it, so it pays to look over the question multiple times. In the case of maths questions, it might help to re-write the question in the answer box if there's space. This means you can look back at it quickly, without making any mistakes.

Don't Hedge Your Bets

Hedging your bets happens when a student tries to give 2 or more answers to a single question, trying to cover as many bases as possible and be less likely to lose marks. After all, if you give lots of different answers, surely one of them is bound to be correct? The problem with this is that examiners will mark harshly against answers like these. Take a look at this example of someone who has tried to hedge their bets:

> *Question: What part of the human body carries blood back to the heart?*

> *Answer: Veins/Arteries*

Only one of the given answers can be correct, since one of them sends blood away from the heart and the other brings blood back to it. The correct answer is "veins", but in this example, both possible answers have been put in. This example answer shows that whoever answered the question wasn't sure, so put both down just in case. Examiners will not award marks for this, so it's essential that you don't try to play it safe in this way. Be confident in your answer.

Avoid Blanking

Have you ever been in a situation where you had something in your head that you were about to say, or about to write, but then completely forgot what it was just before saying or writing it? It can be frustrating in everyday life, but when it happens in an exam it can lead to all kinds of problems. Key details can be forgotten, formulas and tricks may be hard to recall, and sometimes you might just struggle to get off the first page. This is what people refer to as 'blanking'.

Blanking is something that many students worry about, and you've likely heard some horror stories about people who have forgotten everything just as they enter the exam room. However, it doesn't occur as often as you might think, and it doesn't mean you're going to fail your exam.

The best way to prevent blanking is to keep stress to a minimum. This might be easier said than done, but students tend to blank when they haven't had much sleep or have tried to cram their revision into the day before, or the day of the exam itself. This can cause students to panic, and while they're busy worrying, anything that might have been holding in their short-term memory gets forgotten. We'll cover stress in more detail later in this chapter.

In addition to keeping stress to a minimum, make sure that you aren't revising on the day of your exam, and preferably not the night before, either. In order to retain the information in your revision, you need to commit it to what some people call your 'long-term memory'. It takes time for what you've studied to reach this part of your memory, and things revised in the hours before the exam usually haven't made it there. When revision is being held in the short-term memory, you're generally more likely to forget it, which in turn leads to blanking.

If you find that you've blanked in your exam, here are some tips to keep you calm and help you recover from it as quickly as possible:

Take a few deep breaths before continuing. This is important, as you need to stay calm. The more you panic, the less likely you are to remember the information you need. Take a moment to calm down – remember that not performing so well on this exam isn't the end of the world, and that you have the entire paper to remember what you need to know and get back on form.

Look through the question booklet. Sometimes, the wording of a question can jog your memory, or give you a clue of what to write. This can get you started on an answer, which in turn can set off a chain-reaction of memories flooding back, to the point where you remember plenty of information. However, this doesn't always happen; don't rely on this as a replacement for revising over a longer period of time.

Start with an easier question. Some questions require less knowledge than others. If you find yourself blanking in the exam, go onto a question that doesn't need as much precise information as others. Sometimes, a question won't be asking for specific terms or details, but rather an analysis or critical take on the material. These are the questions to do first if you find yourself blanking. This won't work for every kind of exam, however.

Don't attempt any of the larger questions. It might be tempting to just throw caution to the wind and get the toughest or biggest question out of the way. This is usually a bad idea, since these questions contain the most marks. You want to answer these once you've remembered as much as possible, so wait until later in the exam to try them.

It's not the end of the world. If you find yourself running out of time, don't panic. Answer as many questions as you can to secure as many marks as possible. It isn't the end of the world if you don't do so well, and you'll have other exams in which to pick up some marks.

Double-Check Your Work

Everyone makes mistakes. It's almost completely unavoidable, even under relaxed conditions, to create a piece of work that's free of any errors at all. In an exam, you're going to feel a bit rushed, and you're probably going to be working very quickly. This is fine, but remember that you're more likely to make mistakes this way. So, it's important that you go back and check everything you've written. Small, silly errors can cost you big marks, so it's vital to make sure you've fixed anything that could be wrong.

Proofreading can take place at two times during your exam. You can either re-read each of your answers individually after you've completed each one, or you can go back at the end of the exam (if you have time) and check every question in one go. There are benefits and drawbacks to both:

Proofread as you go

Pros	Cons
You're more likely to have time to double-check your answers	If you spend too long proofreading, you might not finish the exam
You can take the exam bit by bit	You might be in "exam-mode" and not be as relaxed as at the end of the exam

Proofread at the end

Pros	Cons
You can focus on finishing the exam first before going back to check	If you take too long doing the exam, you might not have time to proofread towards the end
You'll probably be more relaxed once you've answered all the questions	

Both have pros and cons, and one method may just suit you better. You might prefer the methodical approach of checking every answer once you've finished it. Alternatively, you might find it easier to handle the exam, knowing that you've answered every question that you can, and then go back and check everything in one go.

How to go about proofreading your work will depend on the subject that you're taking, and the questions that you've been asked. If you've had to write essays or other longer bits of text, read over your work, checking for errors. Re-read the question, and make sure that you've answered properly. If you haven't done this, quickly add the extra information in the answer box.

If you've missed something out of an essay, the best thing to do is put a little asterisk symbol (*) where you'd like to add more information. Then, in the next available space (even at the end of the essay), put another asterisk, followed by the information that you've missed out on.

When you double-check your work, you might come across something that you've written, but that you know now is incorrect. In this case, you need to cross it out, so that the person marking your exam knows to ignore these incorrect parts. Put a straight, diagonal line through your work, to indicate any work that you don't want the examiner to look at. Then, all you need to do is replace what you've crossed out with something that's correct.

Bring Some Water and Eat Healthily

You are allowed to bring a bottle of water into almost any

exam. There may be a couple of exceptions for practical-based exams – such as Art, but aside from that, water is allowed. In fact, bringing a bottle of water to drink in an exam is largely encouraged, because it can help you relax and concentrate.

Some studies show that students who take a bottle of water into their exams and drink it get an average score of 5% higher than students who do not. While this might not actually happen for you, this suggests that having a bottle of water handy can be helpful.

On the same topic, eating healthily (and sensibly!) before your exams can make a big difference. Try and avoid drinking fizzy drinks or eating sweets before an exam. The sugar rush might make you feel on top of the world when the exam starts, but you could have a crash halfway through, leaving you shattered for the final stretch. Instead, try and have a good breakfast in the morning before your exams. See what works best for you, but eggs and fish (such as smoked salmon) can give you plenty of energy to complete your exams with.

In addition to this, some exams may allow you to bring in a small piece of food to eat. Fruit is always a safe bet, including bananas and apples. Basically, you want something that doesn't take too long to eat, but gives you enough of a boost to help you through the exam. Remember to check that you're allowed to take food into your exam before doing so.

Stay Healthy

No matter what happens in your exams, it's important

How To Study: Ace Your Grades

that you stay healthy. This is a slightly more general point, but it can't be emphasised enough.

First, you need to stay mentally healthy. Remember that there's life after your exams, and so you shouldn't put yourself under unnecessary pressure. Some anxiety is unavoidable, but it's important that you don't let it get out of control. Between exams, remember to do things that you enjoy, be it sports, video-games, reading fiction, watching television or spending time with friends or family. This will help you to feel calm during your exam period, and remind you that there's more to life than your exams.

Secondly, you need to think about your physical wellbeing. While you're busy revising and making yourself ready to ace the exams, it's easy to forget about your own health. While it's good to take revision seriously, you can't neglect your own physical needs, and so you should make sure to get a lot of the following during your exam period:

- **Sleep.** Everyone needs sleep in order to function, and you're no different! Teenagers and adults need between 8 and 10 hours of sleep per night, so you should be aiming for this as well. A good night's sleep, particularly the night before your exam, can make a world of difference on the day of the test. It will also help you massively during your revision time.

- **A balanced diet.** This can be easily overlooked, but being fed well can be the key to acing an exam on the day. You want to feel as prepared as possible, so be sure to get a good meal the night before and on the day of your exam. Also, try to eat plenty of fruit and vegetables, since they help strengthen your immune system. Some students work themselves extremely hard, then forget to boost their immunity, leading to colds and flu. You want to avoid this – being ill during an exam is horrible!

Planning and Timing Your Exam

Good planning and timing are two of the most important skills that you can learn and practise before sitting your exams. In fact, being able to plan effectively and get your timing down will serve you well in almost every career, so it pays to put the effort in now.

Before you go into your exam, you should find out exactly what the structure of the exam will be.

Try and find out the answers to the following questions:

- How long do I have for the whole exam?
- What type of questions will be asked (essay, single-word answer, short paragraph, problem solving, mathematical sums)?
- How many marks are there in the whole exam?
- Roughly, how many marks are available per question?
- If applicable, how much time is there for planning?

Once you have this information, you can get to work on applying this to your revision schedule. For example, when you attempt a mock exam, you should try to make the situation as close to the real thing as possible. You should plan and time your mock exam as if it were an actual exam. You can find out more about planning and timing your exams in the chapter on subject-specific advice.

Stress

What is Stress?

Stress is an unpleasant sensation that you feel when you're under too much pressure. It's a common feeling to have as a student, especially when studying for and sitting your exams. The pressure that you feel can sometimes grow to become too much to deal with, and can be bad for your physical and mental health, as well as your exam performance.

<u>Stress can be the result of several different worries about your exams. Worries can include:</u>

- Will I get the grades I want/need?
- Have I revised enough?
- Have I left it too late to start revising?
- What will my family and friends think of me if I don't do well?
- What if bad questions show up in my exam?
- What if I oversleep and miss my exam?
- What if I get into the exam hall and forget everything?

Rest assured that, no matter what you're worried about in the run-up to your exams, thousands of other students have felt similar things. It's quite normal to feel a bit stressed during the exam period (if you have more than one). However, it's important to keep these pressures in check, and prevent stress from harming you or your chances of acing your exams. The rest of this section will be devoted to discussing stress, and will hopefully give you some advice on how to manage and prevent it.

How Do I Know If I'm Feeling Exam Stress?

It can be difficult to know if you're stressed or not. Some people are genuinely stressed, but dismiss it as normal – perhaps because they do not know any different. If you're feeling stressed at all, it's important to identify it and make steps against it before stress becomes too much to handle.

The symptoms of stress occur because, when the body is under pressure, it releases hormones which trigger 'fight or flight' responses in the body. In prehistoric times, these symptoms may have proven useful for preparing the body to protect itself from a threat, or be able to run away quickly. Nowadays, we aren't particularly worried about fighting or escaping from wild animals, so the symptoms of stress aren't particularly helpful.

Stress has both emotional and physical symptoms. If you have any of the following symptoms, and feel unable to cope, then you might be stressed:

How To Study: Ace Your Grades

Emotional Symptoms	Physical Symptoms
Low self-esteem	Trouble sleeping
Anxiety	Sweating
Constant worrying	Loss of appetite
Short temper	Loss of concentration
	Headaches
	Dizziness

Whether you think you feel these symptoms or not, keep reading to find some methods for preventing stress, and some ways to reduce the stress that you may already have.

How Can I Prevent Exam Stress?

First of all, remember that exam stress is completely normal for candidates sitting exams. These exams might be very important, and if you're feeling stressed about them it at least shows that you recognise their significance. While stress definitely isn't a good thing, the bright side of it is that you and your body are aware of how important your exams are. Now what's needed is to keep your stress levels down so you can operate at peak performance, and more importantly stay healthy in body and mind!

This section will cover the "dos" and "don'ts" for dealing with exam stress, both during revision and the exams themselves.

DO...

Start revision early. This might seem obvious by now,

but starting your revision earlier in the year is one of the best ways to avoid stress. The more time you have, the less you need to do each day. This gives you more free time, and also allows you to make use of extra time to do other revision activities such as practice papers.

Have a countdown to the end of your exams. Buy a calendar and make note of all your exam dates. Tick days off as they go by, and stay focused on the end. Staying aware of the end point of your exams will remind you that there's life after your exams. There is light at the end of the tunnel.

Listen to your body. At times, you might feel like an unstoppable machine, speeding through revision. During this period, it can be tempting to ignore your bodily needs and soldier on. Likewise, when you're worried about not finishing your revision in time for the exam, it seems like a good idea to stay up all night to make up lost time. Whether you're ignoring your body because you're doing well or poorly, it isn't advisable to do so. You can't function properly without food, water and sleep, so remember to take the breaks in your revision to do these things. That way, when you come back to revising, your study sessions will be more valuable because you're able to focus harder.

Forget about the exam once it's over. It's likely that you'll have more than one exam. You might even have multiple exams on consecutive days, or even on the same day. So, it's important not to linger on an exam once you've finished it. As soon as the exam ends, you have permission to forget about it entirely. Try and avoid talking to others about details of the exam, because it might give you second thoughts about what you wrote in yours. There's no use worrying now since there's no way of changing what you've written. Stay confident and move onto the next exam.

Remember that exams aren't the be-all and end-all. As we've already mentioned, life won't end if you don't get top marks in an exam. You might be disappointed by your grade, but remember that life goes on and your exam results won't ruin your life. What's just as important is a confident and prepared attitude, so even if you don't do as well as you'd hoped to, you should focus on moving forward, learning from your mistakes, and enjoying life.

Ask others for support. No person is an island, and everyone occasionally needs someone else to help them through tough times. Exams can be difficult, and a lot of pressure is put on candidates taking exams, especially academic ones such as GCSE and A-Level. When the going gets tough, don't be afraid to talk to your friends and family. Find people you trust and talk to them about your worries. Sometimes, just talking about things can make you feel calmer, even if you don't figure out any solutions. More often than not, your worries will be amplified by the general worry of exams, and so talking through your problems and rationalising them can be a form of therapy. You might find that your worries are just the result of paranoia, and aren't grounded in reality.

DON'T...

Rely on online forums. The internet can be an excellent

Exam Techniques and Preparation

place to find information and techniques for studying. You have access to plenty of specific advice on a range of subjects, and this can supplement your work in the classroom and your revision at home. However, not all resources are useful, and not all environments on the internet are good for your wellbeing. Some exam-focused chatrooms and forums can do more harm than good. You may come across people who are arrogant about the work that they've done, trying to make you feel worse about your studies as a result. Make use of the internet when it comes to your exams, but try not to linger in places that won't make you feel better about your own studies.

Pay attention to how much revision others are doing. If you are part of a group who is about to take an exam, you'll likely find classmates who are all too willing to let you know how much revision they're doing, and how well their revision is going. These people are probably having a really hard time with their revision, and are just looking for a way to feel better about themselves. If you need to, ignore these people until your exams are over, and instead spend your free time with people who don't stress you out as much.

Get lazy because your friend has done less revision than you. Just as you'll probably come across someone who's apparently done a lot of revision, you probably have a friend or classmate who has apparently done no revision at all, or very little. While they might be telling the truth, it's also possible that they've actually done quite a lot of revision and they claim to have done little in order to look cool. It's tempting to get lazy about your revision because there's someone else who's done less, but remember that exams aren't about how well others are doing: it's about how well **you** are doing. In turn, this could lead to stress as you realise that you haven't done enough just before the exam. Make sure that you avoid getting lazy with your revision, and this will be far less likely to happen.

Set goals you can't meet. Always remember that there's only so much that you can do each day when it comes to revision. If you've put together a revision timetable then this shouldn't be a problem, but double-check how much work you've allotted for each day. During the revision period, take note of how much you're doing each day, and adjust your timetable based on this. For example, if you're finding that 10 topics is far too many, try reducing it to 7 or 8. Likewise, if you're able to do loads more than 5, experiment and see how many topics you get through in one day. The aim of this is to finish each day satisfied that you did everything you can, and that everything is completed. This should work towards preventing exam stress.

Panic about your exam timetable. Occasionally, you might not meet all of your goals for the day. While this isn't a good thing, you need to remember that you always have the next day to cover what you failed to achieve the day before. At the end of your revision for the day, you should try and put yourself in the mind-set that everything is fine – meaning that you can relax and get some quality sleep.

Rely on caffeine or other stimulants. Caffeine will affect your concentration and sleep-patterns. If you become dependent on it, you'll find yourself unable to perform properly without it, which could lead to uncomfortable and unproductive revision sessions. This could cause stress over time, as you require a certain chemical in your body in order to feel ready to study or sit an exam. In addition, interrupting your sleeping-pattern can make you feel tired during your study time, and can cause stress in general. Do yourself a favour and keep away from the caffeine during the exam period.

Conclusion

Exams of any kind can be incredibly difficult. They can test you in all sorts of ways, and generally ask a lot of you in terms of preparation and commitment. However, this is also what makes them so rewarding when you finally succeed. Exams aren't designed to be cruel, but rather find the right person for the role, or otherwise gauge your ability.

Also, bear in mind that you're not the first person to take exams, and you won't be the last either. This means that there have been years of perfecting exam materials, so you shouldn't be too worried about anything unfair coming to the surface while you're completing them.

If there's absolutely one thing that you must take away from this, it's that exams aren't the be-all and end-all in your life. They're certainly important, and you should take them seriously, but don't let yourself become distraught over worries about exams, or results which weren't as high as you might have hoped. There's much more to life than exams.

Improving Your Memory

Up to now, you've learned plenty of tips and tricks for revision and exam success. If you follow all of these steps, you'll do much better than if you hadn't prepared at all. However, there's even more you can do to improve your chances and make sure you're in the best position to ace your exams. In this chapter, we're going to take a look at how to make great use of one of your brain's greatest assets – your memory.

We'll be starting by taking a look at how memory works. With this in mind, we'll then move onto ways of improving your memory. Afterwards, you'll have the opportunity to play some sample memory games, which can be used to see how strong your memory is.

How Does Memory Work?

While neuroscientists haven't uncovered all of the mysteries regarding the brain, the mind, and consciousness, we have a good understanding of how memories are formed and stored in the brain. In this chapter, we'll be taking a look at the physical elements of memory, such as which processes create memories as well as where memories are held. Then, we'll be moving onto helpful ways about thinking of memory and how it works – ways that will hopefully give you a better understanding of where you need to improve in your revision.

Memory – It's all in your Head

While there are still mysteries about memory, neuroscientists have a good idea about how it works. To start with, long-term memories seem to be stored in the hippocampus, a part of the brain. Memories are formed when neurons in the brain make connections with each other – connections that are never broken. There are millions of neurons in your brain, and each will make many connections to other neurons. This means that you'll be able to retain potentially billions of memories during your lifetime. So, you don't really need to worry about running out of space. As far as we can currently tell, short-term memories don't involve any physical changes in the brain – this only occurs when a long-term memory is created.

The reason why it's important to know about how the brain itself deals with memories is that it allows you to find out what lifestyle changes allow for you to improve your memory. In particular, some studies suggest that different foods and activities can stimulate the hippocampus and potentially even strengthen connections made between neurons. While this might not mean that eating certain foods will guarantee a better memory, it might be worth looking into.

Useful Ways to think about Memory

While learning about how the brain works is fascinating and useful in some ways, it isn't entirely helpful just to think of your memory as a billion neurons making connections. Thankfully, some psychologists have specialised in creating models of memory that attempt to describe how it feels for us to create and store memories. While there's some dispute over which model is the most accurate, they can still be helpful ways of thinking about memory so that it's easier to understand.

You might have noticed that, in this book, we've referred to 'short-term' and 'long-term' memory. This is a popular way of thinking about memory, but it isn't entirely accepted across the board by psychologists. Some researchers disagree on whether short-term and long-term memory are two distinct systems in the brain, but instead are a single unit. Whatever the case, it appears that the brain can temporarily hold some memory, and also store it for longer periods of time while also being able to manipulate it to some degree.

So, short-term memory seems to be the place where memories are first stored upon creation. Some people refer to this as 'working memory' since it's the information that you're using in the current moment. There isn't a complete consensus on how much the short-term memory can hold and for how long, but studies show that information in your short-term memory tends to last between 15 and 30 seconds. This is fine when you need to remember a phone number for a few seconds, or remember which cupboard your food goes in, but it isn't particularly useful for remembering large portions of information to recall in an exam. For studying, you really want to make use of your long-term memory.

Long-term memory is different for a number of reasons. Firstly, the creation of long-term memories involves physical changes in the brain. When a long-term memory is formed, more connections are made between the neurons inside your brain. In addition, long-term memory is held permanently, whilst short-term memories can only be held for a limited amount of time. Even if you can't remember it anymore, it's likely that the memories are still in your brain somewhere – you're just having difficulty recalling them.

It might be helpful to think of the long-term memory as a massive hard drive, filled with all kinds of information. Life events, facts, as well as instructions on how to perform certain actions, are all stored in here. As time progresses, you'll gather more memories, meaning that your brain ends up storing a lot of information. Naturally, some memories will be used less than others, and these ones tend to be harder to recall. Essentially, the more you use a memory, the easier it will be to recall. This might be why most revision techniques encourage you to repeat phrases, or recall them on the spot (e.g. flashcards). When revising, bear this in mind – make sure you're recalling all the information you've learned, so that it will be easier to do so in the exam.

It also seems that you're more likely to remember something if you're in an environment that you originally learned it in, or had an experience in. For example, if you first experienced driving in a certain city, you'll likely be reminded of it when you revisit that same place. This means that sitting practice papers in a controlled environment might be useful for remembering things, since sitting in the exam room might jog your memory.

How Can I Improve My Memory?

Your brain can store huge amounts of information, so you don't need to worry about expanding the capacity of your brain. The brain has approximately a billion neurons in it, and each of these can form over one thousand connections to other neurons. This means that there are over a trillion connections in the human brain. If each of these connections accounts for a single memory, then that means your brain can store one trillion memories. If this is true, you don't need to worry about your brain running out of storage space.

Instead, people who want to improve their memory need to focus on the following:

- Making sure information is committed to long-term memory;
- Finding reliable ways to recall these memories easily.

We'll be taking a look at both of these in more detail, looking at tricks which you can use to improve in both areas.

Sending Information to Long-term Memory

As we've discussed, information starts by existing in the short-term memory. This is where memories you need in the moment are kept, and can only last reliably for up to 30 seconds. After this, they either disappear entirely or become inaccurate. For this reason, you need to make sure the information you're absorbing in your revision enters the long-term memory. Lots of things get stored in your long-term memory without much conscious effort on your part, but this doesn't mean you can read a page once and expect it all to be absorbed. You need to focus on the information and use techniques to create strong connections. A lot of people find that associating information with certain things can be useful. Rewriting information in your own words, or discussing it in your own words with a friend, is usually a good way of committing information to long-term memory. You'll associate facts with where you are and who you're talking to, and rewording the information will prove that you understand it.

There are a few other methods, all with some scientific evidence, which allow you to strengthen memories and commit them more easily. Scientists have found a connection between chewing gum while studying and committing more memories to long-term memory, potentially because chewing gum stimulates the hippocampus (the part of the brain which handles memory). Other studies suggest that drinking coffee helps consolidation of information to long-term memory. However, remember that a dependence on caffeine can put you at a disadvantage when you're in the exam room.

Finally, some studies suggest that eating berries can improve your ability to commit information to the long-term memory. This might be worth trying if you want to gain an extra advantage when it comes to studying.

Improving Recollection

Once you've committed things to long-term memory, you need to work on recollection techniques. As previously mentioned, memories that get used often end up being easier to recall. For example, you can probably remember things like your telephone number, home address, or internet passwords easily because you write, say, or type them a lot. Think about your passwords that are saved automatically. When you eventually have to type them in again, are they more difficult to remember? If this is the case for you, then it's because you haven't had to recall it as much.

So, one of the best ways to improve recollection is to test yourself regularly. Almost every revision tactic does this, but the ones that are best suited for this are flashcards, reciting key facts out loud, learning games, and mind maps. Try and do these without looking at your notes so that you can test how strong your ability to recall is.

There are a few other methods which also help to improve recall, including some lifestyle changes. Some studies show that both meditation and exercise can help to strengthen your recall ability. In addition, getting a good night's sleep regularly has been linked to stronger memory. Try these for yourself and see how they work for you.

On top of memories being easier to recall if they're used often, some studies show that creating strong associations between things can make memories easier to recall. For a moment, think of your brain as an attic or large storage locker, and all of the objects inside it represent memories. The ones closest to the entrance are the ones you take out and put back in most regularly, so they're the easiest to recall. However, what about the belongings at the back? Getting to those, or even being able to see them in the darkness, can prove to be incredibly difficult. Now imagine tying a piece of rope to each of these objects, and leaving the loose end near the entrance of the locker. You could follow each of these to find the objects at the back of the room. These pieces of rope represent associations made in your mind, so that these memories are easier to recall. We're now going to take a look at some of the methods you can use to create these associations.

Create Representations in your Brain

This method of making associations is most common, and can be applied to almost any kind of information with a bit of ingenuity. Essentially, you want to give your own meaning to facts and data by representing them in a unique way. For example, if you needed to remember that the Easter Rising in Ireland occurred in 1916, you could imagine a pile of Easter eggs going up in an elevator to floor 1916. This might seem bizarre, but these types of association can help you remember important details more easily. If you're any good at drawing, it might even help to make brief sketches for the most important things you need to know!

Chunking

Chunking is the process of chopping up larger pieces of information into smaller pieces, so that you can remember them more easily. This is particularly useful for things like phone numbers, but can also be used for academic study too. For example, say that you need to memorise a mathematical formula or method for solving a certain kind of maths problem. You could dissect the whole solution into smaller steps, then memorise the process. Then, you can apply the above method for creating representations for each step, or use the method of loci (explained below).

Method of Loci

This is a technique that dates all the way back to the ancient Greeks and Romans, and involves mentally visualising locations and attaching information to them. First, think of a familiar place, such as your bedroom, classroom, or office. Alternatively, you can imagine a route that you take regularly, like your commute to work or school. Then, start to imagine placing the information you need to remember in this environment, such as key dates or names. Once you've done this, try to keep the location in your mind. This means that, when you think of this location, you'll also be able to recall the memories that you've 'placed' there.

Conclusion

In this chapter, we've taken a look at how memory works, as well as ways to improve your memory. In particular, candidates who want to make sure that their memory is at its peak should focus on improving their recollection, since this is what you'll have to rely on under timed conditions in an exam. Make use of the tips above and apply them to the revision methods that we've outlined in our chapter on learning styles. This way, you'll make sure that you're committing as much information as possible to your long-term memory, and creating ways to recall it quickly.

In the next chapter, you'll have the opportunity to try out some memory games for yourself, so you can see how strong your working memory is, as well as test your long-term memory and recollection.

Memory Games

How To Study: Ace Your Grades

All of the methods in the previous chapter are great for strengthening your long-term memory and recollection, but now you have the opportunity to attempt some memory games. These are a great way to test your memory, as well as have a bit of fun.

Sample Memory Games

Remembering Words in Order

In this game, you'll need to remember the order of different words. In the first variation of the game, you'll just need to memorise the order, since you'll be given the list of words at the very end. In later exercises, you'll need to recall the words as well as their order, making things a little more difficult. Try not to look at each exercise for any longer than 30 seconds for the easier questions, and no longer than a minute for the tougher, later questions.

Exercise 1

Memorise the words in the following list:

1	Shotgun
2	Giant
3	Coyote
4	Jade
5	Ghost

How To Study: Ace Your Grades

Now, rearrange the words listed here so they're in the same order as on the previous page:

Giant	Coyote	Jade	Shotgun	Ghost

1	Shotgun ✓
2	Giant ✓
3	Coyote ✓
4	Jade ✓
5	Ghost ✓

Exercise 2

Memorise the words in the following list:

1	Crab
2	Axis
3	Crypt
4	Pancake
5	Apple
6	Garage
7	Salt
8	Jewel
9	Ladybird
10	Glove

134 How To Study: Ace Your Grades

Now, rearrange the words listed here so they're in the same order as on the previous page:

Pancake	Garage	Glove	Salt	Apple
Ladybird	Crab	Crypt	Axis	Jewel

1	Crab ✓
2	Axis ✓
3	Crypt ✓
4	Pancake ✓
5	Apple ✓
6	Garage ✓
7	Salt ✓
8	Jewel ✓
9	Ladybird ✓
10	Glove ✓

Exercise 3

Memorise the words in the following list:

1	Virtual
2	Night
3	Ghoul
4	Power
5	Gadget
6	Dart
7	Jar
8	Injustice
9	Horizon
10	Cyclops

136 How To Study: Ace Your Grades

Now, rearrange the words listed here so they're in the same order as on the previous page:

Jar	Injustice	Ghoul	Horizon	Power
Virtual	Dart	Cyclops	Night	Gadget

1	
2	
3	
4	
5	
6	
7	
8	
9	
10	

Exercise 4

Memorise the words in the following list:

1	Dread
2	District
3	Fierce
4	Leaf
5	Milk
6	Poet
7	Prong
8	Lock
9	Blip
10	Echo

138 How To Study: Ace Your Grades

Now, rearrange the words listed here so they're in the same order as on the previous page:

Lock	Dread	Poet	Milk	Leaf
Echo	Blip	District	Prong	Fierce

1	
2	
3	
4	
5	
6	
7	
8	
9	
10	

Exercise 5

Memorise the words in the following list:

1	Wolf
2	Feet
3	Cola
4	Bin
5	Gymnast
6	Hormone
7	Legend
8	Dove
9	Wilderness
10	Joyride

140 How To Study: Ace Your Grades

Now, rearrange the words listed here so they're in the same order as on the previous page:

Hormone	Cola	Wilderness	Gymnast	Feet
Wolf	Bin	Joyride	Legend	Dove

1	
2	
3	
4	
5	
6	
7	
8	
9	
10	

Exercise 6

For these questions, you need to memorise the words as well their order:

1	General
2	Cat
3	Bar
4	Care
5	Amphibian

142 How To Study: Ace Your Grades

Now, write the words in the order that they appeared on the previous page:

1	
2	
3	
4	
5	

Exercise 7

Memorise the following words, as well as their order:

1	Brawl
2	Glitter
3	Aroma
4	Cottage
5	Captain
6	Cinder
7	Twin
8	Bull
9	Cellblock
10	Gateway

How To Study: Ace Your Grades

Now, write the words in the order that they appeared on the previous page:

1	
2	
3	
4	
5	
6	
7	
8	
9	
10	

Exercise 8

Memorise the following words, as well as their order:

1	Steel
2	Seed
3	Crush
4	Uprising
5	Jump
6	Barbarian
7	Pavement
8	Elimination
9	Faint
10	Bear

How To Study: Ace Your Grades

Now, write the words in the order that they appeared on the previous page:

1	
2	
3	
4	
5	
6	
7	
8	
9	
10	

Exercise 9

Memorise the following words, as well as their order:

1	Plastic
2	Boutique
3	Harmonica
4	Firstborn
5	Beam
6	Archaeology
7	Drive
8	Swamp
9	Angle
10	Lemon

How To Study: Ace Your Grades

Now, write the words in the order that they appeared on the previous page:

1	
2	
3	
4	
5	
6	
7	
8	
9	
10	

Exercise 10

Memorise the following words, as well as their order:

1	Nightfall
2	Wax
3	Skull
4	Annual
5	Goggles
6	Diamond
7	Faith
8	Scar
9	Pill
10	Ceremony

How To Study: Ace Your Grades

Now, write the words in the order that they appeared on the previous page:

1	
2	
3	
4	
5	
6	
7	
8	
9	
10	

Memory Games

Word Recollection Game

For this game, we're going to give you a list of words. Each of these words has been assigned to a number. Your goal in this exercise is to remember both the words and the numbers given to each. Look at the list for a short period of time (no more than 30 seconds for the shorter lists, and no more than a minute for the longer ones), turn the page over and write the words which correspond to each number.

Exercise 1

Memorise the word with its assigned number:

1	Fang
2	Dirt
3	Cloud
4	Phantom
5	Hook

How To Study: Ace Your Grades

Now, without looking at the above list, write the words which correspond to each number:

1	
3	
4	
2	
5	

Exercise 2

Memorise the word with its assigned number:

1	Empire
2	Injury
3	Evil
4	Air
5	Doctor

154 How To Study: Ace Your Grades

Now, without looking at the above list, write the words which correspond to each number:

4	
1	
3	
2	
5	

Exercise 3

Memorise the word with its assigned number:

1	Sword
2	Guest
3	Lottery
4	Savage
5	Bacteria
6	Fist
7	Frost
8	Hamster
9	Rib
10	Airport

156 How To Study: Ace Your Grades

Now, without looking at the above list, write the words which correspond to each number:

6	
10	
3	
8	
4	
2	
5	
7	
9	
1	

Exercise 4

Memorise the word with its assigned number:

1	Alien
2	Gorilla
3	Metal
4	Chief
5	Ankle
6	Barricade
7	Coincidence
8	Badger
9	Escalator
10	Detox

158 How To Study: Ace Your Grades

Now, without looking at the above list, write the words which correspond to each number:

10	
8	
2	
1	
3	
5	
7	
6	
9	
4	

Exercise 5

Memorise the word with its assigned number:

1	Panda
2	Jewel
3	Fuzz
4	Grin
5	Convict
6	Bite
7	Hippopotamus
8	Firm
9	Public
10	Column
11	Hero
12	Fringe
13	Courage
14	Arrow
15	Icicle

160 How To Study: Ace Your Grades

Now, without looking at the above list, write the words which correspond to each number:

3	
10	
5	
1	
9	
15	
12	
14	
8	
6	
11	
2	
7	
4	
13	

Once you're done, head over to the answer section to see how well you did.

Freeform Memory Game – Long-Term Memory

In this section, you have the opportunity to test your long-term memory with information that you need to know. For this section, write down 10 key facts or details that you need to know for your own exam. Then, go away for a few days, and use some revision techniques to remember these key facts. In a week's time, come back to these facts and see how well you remember them.

Fact Number	Fact
1	
2	
3	

How To Study: Ace Your Grades

4	
5	
6	
7	
8	
9	
10	

Sample Memory Games – Answers

Remembering Words in Order

Exercise 1

1	Shotgun
2	Giant
3	Coyote
4	Jade
5	Ghost

Exercise 2

1	Crab
2	Axis
3	Crypt
4	Pancake
5	Apple
6	Garage
7	Salt
8	Jewel
9	Ladybird
10	Glove

Exercise 3

1	Virtual
2	Night
3	Ghoul

How To Study: Ace Your Grades

4	Power
5	Gadget
6	Dart
7	Jar
8	Injustice
9	Horizon
10	Cyclops

Exercise 4

1	Dread
2	District
3	Fierce
4	Leaf
5	Milk
6	Poet
7	Prong
8	Lock
9	Blip
10	Echo

Exercise 5

1	Wolf
2	Feet
3	Cola
4	Bin
5	Gymnast

Memory Games

6	Hormone
7	Legend
8	Dove
9	Wilderness
10	Joyride

Exercise 6

1	General
2	Cat
3	Bar
4	Care
5	Amphibian

Exercise 7

1	Brawl
2	Glitter
3	Aroma
4	Cottage
5	Captain
6	Cinder
7	Twin
8	Bull
9	Cellblock
10	Gateway

How To Study: Ace Your Grades

Exercise 8

1	Steel
2	Seed
3	Crush
4	Uprising
5	Jump
6	Barbarian
7	Pavement
8	Elimination
9	Faint
10	Bear

Exercise 9

1	Plastic
2	Boutique
3	Harmonica
4	Firstborn
5	Beam
6	Archaeology
7	Drive
8	Swamp
9	Angle
10	Lemon

Exercise 10

1	Nightfall
2	Wax
3	Skull
4	Annual
5	Goggles
6	Diamond
7	Faith
8	Scar
9	Pill
10	Ceremony

Word Recollection Game

Exercise 1

1	Fang
3	Cloud
4	Phantom
2	Dirt
5	Hook

Exercise 2

4	Air
1	Empire
3	Evil
2	Injury
5	Doctor

Exercise 3

6	Fist
10	Airport
3	Lottery
8	Hamster
4	Savage
2	Guest
5	Bacteria
7	Frost
9	Rib
1	Sword

Exercise 4

10	Detox
8	Badger
2	Gorilla
1	Alien
3	Metal
5	Ankle
7	Coincidence
6	Barricade
9	Escalator
4	Chief

Exercise 5

3	Fuzz
10	Column
5	Convict
1	Panda
9	Public
15	Icicle
12	Fringe
14	Arrow
8	Firm
6	Bite
11	Hero
2	Jewel
7	Hippopotamus
4	Grin
13	Courage

Conclusion

How To Study: Ace Your Grades

So, you now know all the tips we can give you studying and acing your exams. You've been introduced to several revision techniques, and hopefully had the opportunity to find out what type of learner you are. In addition, you've been given the rundown on exams, and you know how to combat stress. Finally, we've taken a look at human memory – how it works, how to make use of it, and how to improve it to make your revision as effective as possible.

One thing to take away from this book is that exams aren't the most important thing in the world. They might feel like that while you're studying for them, with what feels like a mountain to overcome, but once they're over and you get your results, you should feel satisfied (and proud) of what you've accomplished. Make use of the tips we've provided in this book, try your best, and go away from your exams knowing that you've done something impressive and commendable, no matter the result.

A Few Final Words…

You have reached the end of your guide on how to study. If you have read the information in this book and made use of the tips provided, you should be on your way to passing your exams comfortably and making yourself proud. Hopefully, you will feel far more confident in what you know as well as what you need to improve.

For any test, it is helpful to consider the following in mind…

The Three 'P's

1. Preparation. Preparation is key to passing any test; you won't be doing yourself any favours by not taking the time to prepare. Many fail their tests because they did not know what to expect or did not know what their own weaknesses were. Take the time to re-read any areas you may have struggled with. By doing this, you will become familiar with how you will perform on the day of the test.

2. Perseverance. If you set your sights on a goal and stick to it, you are more likely to succeed. Obstacles and setbacks are common when trying to achieve something great, and you shouldn't shy away from them. Instead, face the tougher parts of the test, even if you feel defeated. If you need to, take a break from your work to relax and then return with renewed vigour. If you fail the test, take the time to consider why you failed, gather your strength and try again.

3. Performance. How well you perform will be the result of your preparation and perseverance. Remember to relax when taking the test and try not to panic. Believe in your own abilities, practise as much as you can, and motivate yourself constantly. Nothing is gained without hard work and determination, and this applies to how you perform on the day of the test.

Good luck with your exams. We wish you the best of luck in all of your future endeavours!

Useful Resources

	Monday	Tuesday	Wednesday	Thursday	Friday	Saturday	Sunday
09:00 - 10:00							
10:00 - 11:00							
11:00 - 12:00							
12:00 - 13:00							
13:00 - 14:00							

	Monday	Tuesday	Wednesday	Thursday	Friday	Saturday	Sunday
14:00 - 15:00							
15:00 - 16:00							
16:00 - 17:00							
17:00 - 18:00							
18:00 - 19:00							

	Monday	Tuesday	Wednesday	Thursday	Friday	Saturday	Sunday
09:00 - 10:00							
10:00 - 11:00							
11:00 - 12:00							
12:00 - 13:00							
13:00 - 14:00							

	Monday	Tuesday	Wednesday	Thursday	Friday	Saturday	Sunday
14:00 - 15:00							
15:00 - 16:00							
16:00 - 17:00							
17:00 - 18:00							
18:00 - 19:00							

	Monday	Tuesday	Wednesday	Thursday	Friday	Saturday	Sunday
09:00 - 10:00							
10:00 - 11:00							
11:00 - 12:00							
12:00 - 13:00							
13:00 - 14:00							

	Monday	Tuesday	Wednesday	Thursday	Friday	Saturday	Sunday
14:00 - 15:00							
15:00 - 16:00							
16:00 - 17:00							
17:00 - 18:00							
18:00 - 19:00							

	Monday	Tuesday	Wednesday	Thursday	Friday	Saturday	Sunday
09:00 - 10:00							
10:00 - 11:00							
11:00 - 12:00							
12:00 - 13:00							
13:00 - 14:00							

	Monday	Tuesday	Wednesday	Thursday	Friday	Saturday	Sunday
14:00 - 15:00							
15:00 - 16:00							
16:00 - 17:00							
17:00 - 18:00							
18:00 - 19:00							

WANT TO IMPROVE YOUR MEMORY AND LEARN EVEN MORE REVISION TRICKS?

CHECK OUT OUR OTHER REVISION GUIDES:

ACHIEVE 100% SERIES
PASS YOUR GCSEs WITH LEVEL 9s
- Expedite your learning
- Improve your memory
- Increase your grade!

HOW2BECOME.COM

ACHIEVE 100% SERIES
PASS YOUR A-LEVELS WITH A*s
- Expedite your learning
- Improve your memory
- Increase your grade!

HOW2BECOME.COM

FOR MORE INFORMATION ON OUR REVISION GUIDES, PLEASE CHECK OUT THE FOLLOWING:

WWW.HOW2BECOME.COM

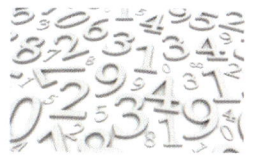

Get Access To

FREE
Educational Tests

www.MyEducationalTests.co.uk

Printed in Great Britain
by Amazon